When it comes to talking about sex, people think they know what Christians are against—but what are they for? In a culture that sees Christianity as shaming and oppressive, it takes an open mind to pick up this book and read it. But for those willing to swim against the flow, Sam Allberry's fresh look at what the Bible says about sex will challenge misconceptions. It could even change your life.

Glynn Harrison MD
Formerly Professor of Psychiatry and Consultant Psychiatrist;
Author, *A Better Story: God, Sex and Human Flourishing*

My generation has grown up in a culture which tells us that the Christian view of sexual expression is not just boring and bizarre but offensive and repressive. Sam's book is a refreshing and insightful reminder that the baby may have got tangled up in the bedsheets. With kindness and clarity, and using a wealth of interesting illustrations, Sam explores some of the unresolved tensions we've inherited from the sexual revolution, and shows how Jesus' life, death and teaching don't just make sense of our longings but meet our deepest needs.

Rachel Jones
Author, *Is This It?*

Clear, wise, pastoral and in places very funny, *Why Does God Care Who I Sleep With?* gives an excellent answer to one of our generation's most pressing questions. If this is a question you've asked, wondered about or even just heard from others, Sam Allberry's brief and thoughtful book will be a great help.

Andrew Wilson
Pastor, Author and Broadcaster

Sam Allberry writes with clarity and empathy about one of the biggest questions of our day. His honesty and sense of humour cut through the stereotypes and platitudes we might be used to hearing about sexual relationships. Here is a countercultural voice challenging us to consider afresh the Christian faith and, ultimately, a relationship with God amid the changing landscape of culture we find ourselves in.

Dr Amy Orr-Ewing
Director, The Oxford Centre for Christian Apologetics

Given all the controversies and challenges surrounding sex, I am delighted to welcome this bold, wise and sensitive treatment of the issues at stake. This is a book capable of changing opinions, altering viewpoints and, ultimately, rescuing lives. Thank you Sam Allberry!

J. John
Pastor, Author and Broadcaster

In this rich and provocative book, Sam Allberry explores how the yearnings of our hearts, the instincts of our bodies and the complex cravings of our minds point us to something we want even more than sex. You can read it in an evening. But its effects could last a lifetime.

Dr Rebecca McLaughlin
Author of *Confronting Christianity:
12 Hard Questions for the World's Largest Religion*

Clear, careful, compassionate and compelling—Sam's analysis of the sexual culture and why it matters to God is a message for every human being. Buy two copies. At least. You'll need them because I guarantee you won't want to pass on your own copy.

Adrian Reynolds
Author and Pastor

Why does God care who I sleep with?

SAM ALLBERRY

Why does God care who I sleep with?
© Sam Allberry, 2020

Published by:
The Good Book Company in partnership with
The Oxford Centre for Christian Apologetics and The Zacharias Institute

thegoodbook.com | www.thegoodbook.co.uk
thegoodbook.com.au | thegoodbook.co.nz | thegoodbook.co.in

Sam Allberry has asserted his right under the Copyright, Designs and Patents Act
1988 to be identified as author of this work.

A CIP catalogue record for this book is available from the British Library.

ISBN: 9781784982775 | Printed in India

Design by André Parker

Contents

To Logan Gates and Ben Dyson,
with thanks for your faithful friendship

Introduction: Christianity's unavoidable problem

It was probably the most bizarre moment of my life.

I was doing some English teaching in central Thailand and had been invited to contribute to a regional training day for high-school English teachers. As a "native" English speaker, I was there to help with things like pronunciation and conversational English. Or so I thought.

The first indication that this wasn't going to go as I'd expected was when they invited me onto the stage at the start of the day. After they introduced me they said we were going to open the day by singing the song chosen as the theme for the day. Or rather, their very own native English-speaking guest was going to.

The bad news: I *really* can't sing, not in front of actual people. The good news: the song was in English. The other bad news: the karaoke system they were using. It was weird enough that it was early morning on a Saturday, that I was in the middle of a very unfamiliar country, that I'd agreed to come and do this as a last-minute favour to my Thai hosts, and that I was now about to sing solo to several hundred teachers.

The song was *I Just Called To Say I Love You* by Stevie Wonder—admittedly a great song, but not necessarily what you'd immediately associate with teaching the language of Shakespeare. I was already well out of my comfort zone, but that wasn't the worst of it. The background footage on the karaoke screen was rather raunchy—a procession of writhing bodies in various states of undress. Somehow I had to follow the words while ignoring the incongruous imagery they were accompanied by. And try not to turn the colour of beetroot while doing it.

All of which is to say that it is impossible to avoid the subject of sex. If it pops up in as innocuous a setting as I was in that morning in Thailand, there really is little hope of steering clear of it in any and every area of life.

And if I'm honest, short of repeating my karaoke experience from that morning, writing a book on sex is about as bizarre a thing as I can imagine myself doing right now. But, like I say, it's impossible to avoid—because it means so much to all of us.

For the past few years I've been working for a charity whose main task is to address the most urgent questions people have about the Christian faith. Other books in this series will give you a feel of what some of those questions are; but top of the list for most people invariably has something to do with what Christians think and believe about sex.

It is not hard to see why. We know that our sexuality, sex, and the relationships we form are a part of life that really matters. It is not inconsequential. I am very conscious that every single one of us has a range of powerful emotions that come into play as we talk, think and react to sex and sexuality in our lives and culture. We have memories (both good and bad) that shape how we think and behave. Some of us will have painful memories and experiences that continue to haunt us. Some of us will be restless, seeking some form of deeper satisfaction than we're currently experiencing. Some of us will be confused by various things we've experienced. And some of us will be perfectly happy with our sex life as it is, and perhaps wonder what all the fuss is about.

And that means that this could be a difficult book for you to read. Whether you're a Christian or not, you may at times find yourself wanting to grunt in disgust or hurl the book across the room—because what I am suggesting conflicts so deeply with your own views and experience.

But rather than give in to your instinct to hurl this book far from you, can I urge you to consider carefully, and as objectively as you can, as I try to explain why I think sex matters so much to all of us. I'm writing this as someone who is single and expects to remain so for the future. As a Christian that means I am committed to being celibate—to *not* having sex unless it is with someone I'm married to. This issue matters to me, just as it does to us all.

DANGEROUS

There are significant challenges for Christians in discussions about sex. More and more, sexual freedom is regarded as one of the greatest goods in Western society. A huge amount has changed over the past decade or so. Just fifteen years ago Christians like me, who follow the teaching of the Bible, would have been thought of as old-fashioned for holding to the traditional Christian understanding of sex being exclusively for marriage.

But now, increasingly, we are thought of as being dangerous to society. Our views on sex have become *that* significant. Who we sleep with is seen as a supreme human right.

Anything that seems to constrain our choice in this area is somehow viewed as an existential threat.

So the Christian claim that sex is for a very particular context is far more of an offense than it is a curiosity. *Why should God care who I sleep with?* is perhaps less a question and more just a freestanding objection that doesn't really require an answer.

And yet an answer exists. Christians continue to believe what we believe about sex, and it is a belief that isn't going away, however much it might be derided today. And it is a belief for which there are compelling reasons. I would love you to understand these reasons and weigh them properly before you decide what to do with them.

God cares who we sleep with because he cares deeply about the people who are doing the sleeping. He cares because sex was his idea, not ours. He cares because misusing sex can cause profound hurt and damage. He cares because he regards us as worthy of his care. And, in fact, that care is not only seen in telling us how we should use sex, but also in how he makes forgiveness and healing available to us when we mess this up.

A quick word about the title: Yes, *Why does God care about with whom I sleep?* <u>is</u> more grammatically correct, but it's clunky, and I really think God (and we) have bigger things to worry about. Start on the next page and you'll see what I mean.

Why do we care who we sleep with?

I t's not often that a single tweet explodes into a whole movement.

In late 2017 Hollywood was ablaze with a series of accusations against one of its most celebrated producers, Harvey Weinstein. A succession of women were accusing him of predatory behaviour, and it was receiving widespread attention. On October 15 one actress, Alyssa Milano, tweeted the following:

> If you've been sexually harassed or assaulted write "me too" as a reply to this tweet.

The hashtag *#MeToo* quickly went viral. The original tweet was posted around noon and by the end of the day the phrase "Me too" had been used on Twitter over 200,000 times. Within a year, it had been used 19 million times—more than 55,000 each day.[1]

Many celebrities also told their stories, further raising the profile of the hashtag. Hollywood was engulfed. Other

---

1   *USA Today:* go to. www.bit.ly/occasleep (accessed 21 August 2019).

parts of the entertainment industry followed. Stories of harassment and abuse quickly spread in the realms of politics, media, academia and religion. A parallel *#ChurchToo* hashtag began to emerge as survivors of assault in churches or by church leaders shared their own experiences.

Although Milano's tweet seemed to be the starting gun for this, she was not the first person to use the phrase "me too" in this context (as she went on to acknowledge). The hashtag's true origin had been a decade earlier. Activist Tarana Burke was "looking for a succinct way to show empathy", according to an interview in the *Huffington Post*. "Me too is so powerful because somebody had said it to me and it changed the trajectory of my healing process once I heard that." Soon after Milano's tweet went viral, Burke herself wrote, "The point of the work we've been doing over the past decade with the 'me too movement' is to let women, particularly young women of colour, know that they are not alone".[2]

The widespread adoption of the hashtag has certainly had that effect. Young women of colour may have been a particular concern for Burke, but the hashtag has also enabled many others—women of different backgrounds and ages, along with some men too—to be able to share their stories.

One story is particularly worth reflecting on. Writing in *The Atlantic*, Caitlin Flanagan spoke of the time at high school when a young man had attempted to rape her in his car at an empty parking lot by a beach. After a struggle he eventually stopped and drove her home. She never spoke about it, and goes on in the article to explain why:

---

2 *Huffington Post*. www.bit.ly/occasleep2 (accessed 21 August 2019).

I told no one. In my mind, it was not an example of male aggression used against a girl to extract sex from her. It was an example of how undesirable I was. It was proof that I was not the kind of girl you took to parties, or the kind of girl you wanted to get to know. I was the kind of girl you took to a deserted parking lot and tried to make give you sex. Telling someone would not be revealing what he had done; it would be revealing how deserving I was of that kind of treatment.[3]

The *#MeToo* movement has shone a spotlight on the prevalence of sexual assault. It is now thought that between 20% and 30% of American women have been sexually assaulted in the course of their lives. Exact figures are hard to come by; these are extremely difficult stories for people to share, for a host of reasons, as Flanagan's story highlights. But many have been able to open up for the first time, and we are gaining a truer understanding of the prevalence of these brutalities. Men too are opening up about their experiences of sexual assault and harassment. Some men are also acknowledging failures in their own past behaviour towards women. On all sorts of levels, from individuals to institutions, the western world seems to be having a major reassessment of its collective sexual values.

If *#MeToo* has shown us anything, it is that our sexuality matters profoundly. Its violation leads to the deepest emotional and psychological damage, quite apart from the physical scars it leaves. Flanagan's own story reflects this so powerfully. What that young man attempted to do to her told her something about herself, and her worth, that became calcified in her thinking over many years afterwards.

---

3   *The Atlantic.* www.bit.ly/occasleep3 (accessed 21 August 2019).

JESUS ON ABUSE

We might wonder at this point how any of this connects to Christianity. If anything, Christianity seems to be just as much a part of the problem as any other movement, and perhaps even more so. As more and more historic and present-day accusations are proved, it is very clear that many Christian institutions have been places of horrific abuse. In any context, these facts would be appalling. But it's the Christian context that makes them all the more reprehensible. We all know that sexual assault is wrong; no one group or religion has a monopoly on that conviction. But Christians have more reason than perhaps anyone else to know that.

Jesus of Nazareth, the founder of Christianity, was known for his care for the marginalised, for the overlooked and for the vulnerable. It was said of him, "A bruised reed he will not break" (Matthew 12 v 20); he was someone who was naturally tender towards the wounded and hurting. There is something particularly incongruous, therefore, about those who purport to follow Jesus who contradict his teaching and example on this point.

But it is also worth noting that Jesus was himself the victim of unimaginable abuse. We don't need to be Bible-believing Christians to know the basic facts about how the life of this man ended. The historical record shows us that he was publicly executed by the Roman authorities on the orders of Pontius Pilate.[4] We know he was killed by crucifixion. We also know that this followed a grueling process of humiliation and torture. The New Testament accounts are surprisingly light on the gory details but tell us that

---

4   See, for example, John Dickson, *Is Jesus History?* (The Good Book Company, 2019), p 149-154.

Jesus was stripped, flogged, beaten and mocked. He was sexually exposed, physically abused, and repeatedly ridiculed. His own companions betrayed him, denied him or deserted him. The emotional, psychological and physical suffering is not something we can easily quantify. All this was before he even arrived at the point of crucifixion.

This is the man Christians follow and worship. And that tells us that Christians should have an inbuilt sensitivity towards those who are victims. Because Jesus himself embodied and experienced some of the most intense forms of victimisation and rejection, an awareness of pain and brutality is baked into Christianity. Christians should be the last people on earth to show indifference to abuse, let alone enabling or perpetrating it in any way. This is reinforced by Jesus' own teaching about human sexuality.

JESUS ON SEX

One of the best-known sections of Jesus' teaching is the Sermon on the Mount. Many of its lines have become embedded in Western culture. You might be more familiar with it than you'd thought. Jesus touches on the issue of sexual ethics early on in the sermon:

> *You have heard that it was said, 'You shall not commit adultery.' But I tell you that anyone who looks at a woman lustfully has already committed adultery with her in his heart.* MATTHEW 5 v 27-28

Jesus knows that his hearers have been taught the Ten Commandments from the Old Testament, including the seventh commandment against adultery (which he quotes). Adultery is any sexual intercourse between a married person and someone who is not their spouse. Jesus reiterates this commandment and adds his own take on it. His words are not in contrast to the content of the commandment but provide fresh insight into how it is meant to be applied.

Make no mistake, what Jesus is saying here is revolutionary, both for the time in which Jesus was speaking and for us today.

Let's think about how these words would have been heard by his original listeners. Jesus was a first-century Jew speaking to an audience of fellow Jews, and the Ten Commandments were foundational to all their ethical thought. They were treated as the executive summary of the whole of God's law in the Old Testament. They continue to exert significant cultural influence today as a basis for morality.

Jesus quotes the seventh commandment against adultery. This was the basis of the shared sexual ethic of that time. We can imagine a Jewish man listening to Jesus. Perhaps he had been faithfully married for many years and felt proud of how he had conducted himself. Perhaps he was one of the first to disapprove of adultery whenever he ever heard about others involved in it. Maybe it would never even occur to him to get into a situation where he might end up being physically intimate with another woman. His hands had never touched any woman other than his wife. He would have been typical of many, committed to this commandment and confident that he had been fully obedient to it.

So as Jesus says the first part of his teaching—"You have heard that it was said, 'You shall not commit adultery'"—men like this would have nodded along with enthusiasm. *Yes, this is what we've always heard. This is what we've always stood by.* They may have found other aspects of Jesus' teaching challenging or searching (it is hard to read through the Sermon on the Mount without experiencing this), but on this point they could feel sure that they would meet his full approval.

But then comes the second part of what Jesus says:

> *But I tell you that anyone who looks at a woman lustfully has already committed adultery with her in his heart.*

Think about that. Jesus is not contradicting how people had understood the commandment; he's expanding what it means and how it applies. They'd assumed it was just about physical adultery. But physical adultery is not the only kind there is; Jesus is saying adultery can take place in hearts even if it never takes place in beds. It can be committed by looking, not just by touching—*anyone who looks with lustful intent has already committed adultery.* It is not simply about what you do with your genitals but what you do with your eyes and your mind—how you look and think about another person.

Jesus is concerned with *intent.* His issue is not with people noticing each other, but with people looking at others "with lustful intent." It is the difference between noticing that someone is attractive and wanting in some way to have them. *That,* Jesus says, is what the commandment against adultery is getting at. We'll return to the significance of this in due course.

THE VICTIM

But while Jesus' main focus is on the person doing the looking, it is worth pausing to think about what this implies about the person being looked at.

Jesus gives us a scenario where a man is looking lustfully at a woman. What Jesus is teaching here applies to us all, of course, but it may be that men in particular need to hear it.

After all, the overwhelming majority of sexual violations are committed against women rather than men.

So Jesus says the man looking lustfully at a woman has broken the commandment against adultery just as surely as if he had physically slept with her.

But think about what Jesus is also saying about the woman. *She is not to be looked at lustfully.* Jesus is saying that her sexuality is precious and valuable: that she has a sexual integrity to her which matters and should be honoured by everyone else. *He is saying that this sexual integrity is so precious that it must not be violated, even in the privacy of someone else's mind.* Even if she were never to find out about it, she would have been greatly wronged by being thought about lustfully.

We tend to think that someone's thought life is their business alone, and that what they think about in their own head has nothing to do with anyone else; and so we might want to write Jesus off at this point for daring to regulate what goes on in our minds. But before we do, we need to see *why* Jesus is saying this. As someone once said, we shouldn't take down a fence until we know the reason it was put there in the first place.[5] Jesus is showing us that our sexuality is far more precious than we might have realised, and that his teaching is actually a form of protection for it.

NOT JUST JESUS

Jesus' teaching reflects something we see throughout the whole Bible: how we treat one another sexually matters a great deal to God.

One of Israel's greatest heroes in the Old Testament was King David. He united the kingdom, defeated many enemies (fa-

---

5 G. K. Chesterton, "The Thing," *The Collected Works of G.K. Chesterton, Vol 3* (San Francisco: Ignatius Press, 1986) p 157.

mously including the giant Goliath) and was a skilled poet and musician. But the Bible never whitewashes its heroes. It paints them with all their flaws and faults. And for David, his flaws led to an infamous incident with a woman called Bathsheba.

We'll come back to this episode a couple of times in this book, as David is a foundational example of just how messed up things can get, and also of how we can find healing and forgiveness from God in the context of even terrible mistakes.

David summoned one of his subjects, Bathsheba—a married woman—to sleep with him. She became pregnant, and so he arranged for her military husband, Uriah, to have some time back home with her from the battlefield, so that people would assume the baby belonged to Uriah. This didn't work, so David arranged for Uriah to be killed in battle and quickly married Bathsheba himself.

Sometime after this a brave man called Nathan confronts David about the evil he has committed. David is brought to his senses. The depth of his own wickedness sinks in. He is deeply and rightly remorseful. It is worth noting that he was still the king. This was not the remorse of someone who had been exposed and brought down; he is still on his throne. He could have Nathan killed. It is his own conscience before God, not public opinion or a threat to his career, that leads him to repent.

David writes a powerful poetic prayer to God in which he comes to terms with what he has done. At one point he writes:

> *Against you, you only, have I sinned and done what is*
> *evil in your sight.* PSALM 51 v 4

At first glance this feels very inadequate. It sounds as though

David is conveniently overlooking the human cost of his actions and simply writing it off as "a spiritual matter" between himself and God. It feels evasive, as if he is not properly facing up to the full extent of what he has done.

But the opposite is in fact the case. David realises that what he has done to Bathsheba is a sin against God precisely because *her sexual integrity is something God has given her.* David's violation of Bathsheba is no less than treason against God. Far from minimising the seriousness of his sin against Bathsheba and Uriah, David's prayer is *accounting* for it.

Here's another way of saying this: *any sexual assault is a violation of sacred space.* To mistreat someone is to mistreat something God has made. Other people are not some irrelevant third party: they are people whom God decided to make and cares deeply about. An abuse of them is an affront to him.

This belief gives us a basis for saying that sexual assault is objectively and universally wrong, because it locates the reason in who the victims are to God. He made them. Their personal and sexual integrity matters to him. You mess with them, and you end up picking a fight with God himself. This is what Jesus himself is warning us about in his teaching against adultery.

Who we sleep with matters. Even who we *think* about sleeping with matters. If God cares about us, he will care about our sexuality. It is precious. And a violation of it is serious, as we are about to see.

What is a
little girl worth?

Rachael Denhollander rose to prominence during the trial of Larry Nassar. Nassar, the USA gymnastics national team doctor and a former osteopathic physician at Michigan State University, was on trial for the sexual assault of dozens of young women and girls.

Denhollander gave an impact statement at the trial, excerpts of which went viral online. At the heart of her statement to the judge was one searching question, *What is a little girl worth?*

> *I ask that you hand down a sentence that tells us that what was done to us matters, that we are known, we are worth everything, worth the greatest protection the law can offer, the greatest measure of justice available.*
>
> *And to everyone who is watching, I ask that same question, how much is a little girl worth?*

She concluded with these words:

> *Judge Aquilina, I plead with you as you deliberate the sentence to give Larry, send a message that these victims*

*are worth everything. In order to meet both the goals
of this court. I plead with you to impose the maximum
sentence under the plea agreement because everything is
what these survivors are worth.*[6]

What is a little girl worth? It's a question to which Jesus gives
an unambiguous answer. They are precious—priceless, even.
And therefore their sexual integrity matters enormously to
him. Jesus says what he says about sex in the Sermon on the
Mount not because he has a low view of sex but a very high
view of human sexuality.

It has often been the case that people have written off
Christianity because of its supposedly prudish view of such
matters. But what if the reality was, in fact, the opposite?
What if our sexual integrity was actually far more precious
than we ever realised?

One writer has compared how we view sexuality to our
attitude to having different types of car—the more valuable
the car, the better we aim to take care of it.[7]

I can relate to this. A year or so ago I spent a semester
as a visiting faculty member at an American university and
needed a car to get around. A friend kindly offered me the
use of his old truck any time I wanted it, which was generous if a little reckless. I'm British and had never driven
in the States before, so there was the constant risk that I'd
launch out on the wrong side of the road.

But it turned out not to be that great a risk—not because my
driving skills were any better than expected but because of the
state of the truck. It was old, really old, and had long exceeded

---

6   You can read the entirety of Denhollander's extraordinary impact statement on
    CNN here: www.bit.ly/occasleep4 (accessed 21 August 2019).

7   John Dickson, *A Doubter's Guide to the Ten Commandments* (Zondervan, 2016),
    p 135.

its life expectancy. It didn't really matter what happened to it. It really wasn't worth much to my friend, so as far as he was concerned, I could throw it around and have some fun with it. Another dent, scratch or blown gasket wouldn't make much difference at this stage.

The offer was, nevertheless, still generous and I was grateful for it. I'd have gladly accepted but for a significant factor: another staff member had offered me use of an alternative car, and this one was a beautiful convertible. I couldn't believe it. Let's just say that with this car it really *did* matter how I drove it. It was worth way more than the truck. There wasn't a scratch anywhere to be seen, and I needed to keep it that way. It deserved a huge amount of care.

In other words, being particularly careful about something is often a sign of its special worth, and how much we value it. If I, as a Christian, am particular about how I use my body, you might think it's because I have a low view of physical intimacy—because I think it is disgusting or demeaning in some way. Actually it's because I think of bodies—mine, yours and everyone's—like convertibles, not like beat-up trucks.

I'm particular about physical intimacy not because I value it *so little*, but because I value it *so much*.

HOW WE HAVE FAILED

But this view of human sexuality has not always been understood or accurately reflected by Christian believers. The stereotype of Christians being prudish and negative about sex has some basis in experience, because it has been perpetuated by some Christians over the years.

One example comes from the Middle Ages. Church authorities forbade sex on Thursdays (the day on which Christ was arrested), on Fridays (the day of Christ's death), on Saturdays (in honour of the Virgin Mary), and on Sundays (in honour of the departed saints).[8] It is hard to avoid the impression that Christian leaders at this time really just didn't like people having sex. I can imagine some of them furiously trying to think up reasons to abstain from sex on Mondays, Tuesdays and Wednesdays as well.

Hardly anyone would go that far today, but it is still the case that many in the church seem to have the belief that sex is somehow just *wrong*. But this is simply wrong thinking.

Some time ago I gave a talk at church on a Bible passage about sex, and a concerned church member came up to me afterwards to say that he thought sex was not an appropriate subject for discussion on a Sunday morning. I tried to point out to him that the Bible itself is full of talk about sex and sexuality, and that this passage—along with the whole letter it was part of—would have been originally read out loud to the church to which it was addressed. The Bible is frequently less prudish than some of its ardent readers.

But while some Christians might still take this line, the Bible is emphatically *not* against sex—quite the opposite.

Something of the Bible's more balanced view is seen in the teaching of the apostle Paul, author of much of the New Testament. In one of his letters to a church in a city called Thessalonica, in present-day Greece, Paul starts to outline some of the implications of the Christian faith for everyday life, and he begins with the area of human sexuality:

> *It is God's will that you should be sanctified: that you should avoid sexual immorality.*
>
> 1 THESSALONIANS 4 v 3

---

8   See Philip Yancey, *Designer Sex* (InterVarsity Press, 2003), p 7.

This one verse actually sums up the biblical view of sex. Paul does not say, *Avoid all sexual behaviour*, as though sex itself was a problem and Christians should just avoid it.

This is significant. Christians *do* have a category of sexual behaviour that they believe is wrong. (Actually, *all of us* do, as we'll see.) But there are also forms of sexual behaviour regarded in the Bible as thoroughly good and right. In fact, the Bible *celebrates* these forms of sexual intimacy; it is not at all prudish in the way many people imagine. Sex in these contexts is to be enthusiastically enjoyed. Contrary to popular opinion, Paul is *not* against sex.

But he *is* prohibiting *some* forms of sex. *Some* forms of sexual behaviour are to be avoided. Paul says there is such a thing as "sexual immorality", and he urges his readers to avoid it altogether.

RESTRICTIONS AND FREEDOMS

Many people might roll their eyes at this. Maybe this is what we suspected all along: that Christianity is really far more about sexual restriction than sexual freedom. What right do Christians have to regulate what anyone does in the privacy of their own bedrooms?

But a moment's reflection shows us that *all of us* believe in some form of sexual restriction. Even the most dedicated proponents of sexual freedom acknowledge that *some* boundaries are necessary; it's just that these boundaries are so often assumed, and we don't necessarily recognise that they're there and that they're boundaries.

Take the issue of consent, for example. It's easy to think that the need for consent is so obvious that it barely needs to be stated. When I've suggested that the necessity for consent is a reason why we can't simply say, "Everyone should be allowed to do what they want", the response is often something along the lines of, "Well of *course* we need consent—that's *obvious*".

But the *#MeToo* movement is evidence that this is not so. The need for consent is a boundary we've assumed and now see we need to properly define and enforce.

We only now seem to have become aware of the ways in which, overtly or subtly, people have been pressurised into sexual acts they did not want to participate in. University campuses are having to stipulate precisely what constitutes legal consent: that clear verbal assent must be given at each deepening stage of physical intimacy.

And even with verbal consent, we are conscious of how power dynamics can be at play. If a Hollywood mogul suggests to a struggling young actress that they have some kind of sexual encounter, it is clear that this is not a level playing field. The one has control over the fortunes and success of the other. Even if she gives verbal consent, there is a high probability that it is not genuine if she feels as though this is something the future success of her career is going to depend on.

One of the accusers of the producer Harvey Weinstein put it like this:

> *I am a 28-year-old woman trying to make a living and a career. Harvey Weinstein is a 64-year-old world-famous man, and this is his company. The balance of power is me: 0, Harvey Weinstein: 10.* [9]

So it will not do to simply say that restrictions on someone's sexual desires are backward and unnecessary. Someone's sexual desires may be for coercion and forcing themselves upon

---

9   *New York Times:* www.bit.ly/occasleep5 (accessed 21 August 2019).

someone else. That may be their predominant expression of sexuality. But that is no license to express it. Something else matters more than that person's freedom to fulfil their sexual desires. There is always a need for some kind of external constraint upon sexual behaviour.

The other boundary we commonly assume to be necessary is that consenting parties be adults. We recognise that there is a vulnerability to those who are minors such that, even if consent is given, it cannot be assumed to have been obtained without some kind of coercion or manipulation. And so we rightly put legal boundaries around sexual contact even with older teenagers who are not yet full adults. Again, recent revelations of the sexual abuse of children have shown us that this boundary can never be assumed.

WHERE ARE THE BOUNDARIES?

So, in general, we *don't* believe in unfettered sexual freedom as much as we sometimes claim to. The issue is not whether there should be restrictions on what someone can do sexually but what those restrictions are. All of us believe in the need for them; the issue is what they should be. All of us agree that there is such a thing as sexually immoral behaviour. Not every sexual desire is equally healthy, noble, or right. Some forms of sexual behaviour are harmful. *Everyone* needs to have some level of self-control over their sexual desires.

What is distinctive about the Christian understanding of sexual ethics, then, is not the presence of boundaries but where those boundaries are located and for what reason. The issue is not that Christians are in favour of sexual repression and others are champions for sexual freedom. No one is for full sexual freedom, and everyone believes certain sexual desires should be resisted. What we need to do is look at each set of boundaries and evaluate how compelling the rationale given for them is. Looser boundaries are not necessarily better, just as narrower ones are not necessarily worse. To write off the Christian understanding of sexual ethics as simply being "restrictive" is disingenuous.

Our recent growing awareness of the prevalence and consequences of sexual assault only underlines the importance of boundaries. We are concerned with boundaries precisely because we're convinced that sexuality matters, and that its abuse also matters. This is not prudishness but protection.

NOT JUST PHYSICAL

That certain boundaries are necessary shows us something else: we don't really mean it when we talk about sex being something that's just physical.

In 1999 Bloodhound Gang released the track *The Bad Touch*. Its main lines were…

> *You and me baby ain't nothin' but mammals.*
> *So let's do it like they do on the Discovery Channel.* [10]

We sometimes tend to think this way: that when it comes to sex, we're just animals. We're just obeying the same physical instincts for mating that we share with the rest of the natural world. So why be so precious about it? But we know it is not really true. In every single other area of life we say the exact opposite to one another: "Don't act like such an animal". Whatever we believe about what sets us apart from the beasts, it clearly needs to apply to sex as much as anything else.

In the 2001 Ron Howard movie *A Beautiful Mind*, Russell Crowe plays the brilliant but socially awkward mathemati-

---

10   Lyrics by James M. Franks. I'm grateful to Glen Scrivener for pointing this out to me.

cian John Nash. At one point he meets an attractive woman at a bar, and he clearly doesn't know what to say.

"Maybe you want to buy me a drink?" she suggests.

Nash replies:

I don't exactly know what I'm required to say in order for you to have intercourse with me, but could we assume that I said all that? Essentially we're talking about fluid exchange, right?

As far as he is concerned, this is just about a physical transaction, so they can afford to dispense with the preamble and just agree to have sex. It is no more than "fluid exchange", as if it was no more significant than a handshake.

But this way of thinking is clearly wrong. We are not just animals. Sex is not just physical. However much we have in common with the animal world, it is clear we have different expectations of what sex should involve. Just because certain things happen in nature, and just because we too are creatures, it doesn't mean we can behave in any way we observe in nature and expect it to work. We may be animals to some extent, but we are also much more than that. What may just be physical for animals is often something far more significant for us.

Nash discovers this the painful way. After he suggests that sex is essentially "fluid exchange", the woman slaps him in the face and walks out. As an audience our sympathies are with her. Nash was unable to comprehend something profound and vital.

The fact is, that we care enormously about who we sleep with. Our instincts tell us it matters. Experience (our own or that of others) shows that sexual harassment and assault affects us very deeply, as the harrowing accounts of Caitlin

Flanagan and so many others have shown us. It is undeniably the case that sex involves so much more than our bodies. Sexual activity is not trivial. So much seems to be at stake in how human sexuality is approached that it is fair to say that there really is no such thing as casual sex. Writer and speaker Glen Scrivener pointed out to me once that the pain of sexual assault is not the pain of a grazed knee but the trauma of holy space being desecrated. Maybe our bodies are less like playthings and more like temples.

And we can sense these things. Sometimes experience forces us to confront them. Surprising as it may seem, the Bible has the resources to help us truly account for these feelings and experiences. It is incontrovertible that it matters who we sleep with. The Christian faith, more than anything else, shows us why this is—because it matters deeply to our Creator.

What is sex for?

On any given day there seems to be more than enough in the world to be concerned by.

Just a quick glance at a news app today reminds me there is huge political instability on both sides of the North Atlantic, a growing belligerence from one or two geo-political heavy-weights on the other side of the globe, alarm about the state of the environment and the potential human cost, the usual economic challenges at home and abroad, and the constant and tragic presence of conflict, injustice and exploitation. We're not short of weighty matters to occupy our minds.

So it might seem strange that a particular new concern has been gaining publicity over the last several months: it turns out that *young people are having significantly less sex these days*. It's been dubbed "the sex recession". *The Atlantic* recently reported that "in the space of a generation, sex has gone from something most high-school students have experienced to something most haven't". It continues, "People now in their early 20s are two and a half times as likely to be abstinent as Gen Xers were at that age; 15 percent report having had no sex since they reached adulthood". *The Economist* similarly notes,

> *The portion of Americans aged 18 to 29 who claim to have had no sex for 12 months has more than doubled in a decade—to 23% last year.*[11]

This apparent downward trend in sexual activity has concerned researchers, who fear it may be an indicator of a deeper malaise in this emerging generation.

It has also come as something of a surprise. After all, Western society is thought to be more sexually relaxed and tolerant than ever before. Smartphone technology has also ensured that sex—real and virtual—is more accessible than anyone would have imagined even a few years ago. And yet, by most accounts, teens are much less sexually active than they were 25 years ago. We seem to live in a time where we care about sex more but engage in it much less.[12]

Needless to say, researchers are working to identify factors that might account for this trend. Fingers are being pointed in various directions: everything from crushing economic pressures, growing rates of anxiety or the increasing distraction of streaming services like Netflix to the ubiquity of digital porn, hook-up culture, current health patterns, hesitancy over how to conduct romantic relationships in a *#MeToo* culture, and helicopter parenting.

Whatever the causes, no one seems to be denying the reality. Attitudes to sex are changing, and we don't always know in which direction. Things could look very different even

---

11 *The Atlantic*, December 2018. www.bit.ly/occasleep6 (accessed 21 August 2019).

12 Though the concern primarily seems to be focused on younger people—those who might otherwise be expected to have higher rates of sexual activity—it is also true of adults too. Over the past decade or so the average American adult has gone from having sex 62 times a year to 54 times.

a few years from now. Even if we can't pinpoint the reasons for it, there seems to be less and less motivation among younger people to have sex.

And yet, in a context where the only sex more and more people are interested in is virtual sex or the performed sex of porn and explicit TV, the Bible gives us unembarrassed and positive reasons to value *actual* sex. We've already seen that the caricature of Christianity being anti-sex is inaccurate, at least as far as Scripture is concerned. It matters to us who we sleep with, and it turns out it matters to God too. We need to see why. And the answer might surprise you.

WHY ACTUAL SEX ACTUALLY MATTERS

The starting point is to realise that sex matters to God because people do. The very first chapter of the Bible makes this clear, where we see the account of how God made the world.[13] The words are not dry reportage so much as a joyful *celebration* of God at work in creation—there is rhythm and poetry in the words. We see God forming and filling this world, and it all reaches a crescendo with the arrival of humanity:

> *Then God said, "Let us make mankind in our image, in our likeness, so that they may rule over the fish in the sea and the birds in the sky, over the livestock and all the wild animals, and over all the creatures that move along the ground."*

---

13 There are lots of good questions about how much is being historically and scientifically affirmed in this passage. Such questions are great to ask but take us too far from the subject of this book. A great starting point on this might be John Lennox, *Can Science Explain Everything?* (The Good Book Company, 2019).

> *So God created mankind in his image,*
> *in the image of God he created them;*
> *male and female he created them.*

GENESIS 1 v 26-27

These words may be familiar, and to many the idea that people are made in God's image may seem self-evident. But we need to notice a couple of things that are going on here.

So far in the account of how God created the world, the acts of creation have taken place by God's verbal command: "Let there be light", for example. God announces it, and it happens. He just declares things into existence. This is the case with everything from night and day, land and sea, the sun and moon, plants, animals, fish and birds.

But not people.

When it comes to making us, there seems to be a moment of deliberation. God doesn't just say, "Let there be people", as though they would be a nice accessory for creation. He says, "Let *us* make..." This immediately suggests he's about to make something special, as though he is more invested in this particular act of creation.

WHY YOU ARE SPECIAL

We don't wait long to find out why. What accounts for the special introduction to this act is that God is about to make something in his "image" or "likeness". Genesis 1 shows us that humans are like everything else in the world in that we are created by God and dependent on him for our life, but also (and importantly) unlike *everything else* in the world in that we uniquely reflect something of what God is like. Dogs, dolphins, delphiniums and the Dolomites are all wonderful, but we are the only ones made in the image of God.

This is foundational for how we are to think about every aspect of our lives as people, and the implications are endless. For starters, it means that the person who just pulled out into the road in front of me, causing me to slam on my brakes and send the contents of my car all over the dashboard, is actually someone (despite this particular act) who is more like God than any other kind of creature on the face of the globe. They might look ordinary to me. But they are not. No one is. All of us have inestimable worth in the eyes of God. He made us to reflect something of what he is like. All life is a gift of God. But human life has distinct and unique worth.

There is something sacred about human life. Most of us sense this. We're not indifferent to the welfare of other creatures, and rightly so. But we know that human life matters in a unique way. When someone treats a pet like a human, we think it a little odd. But when someone treats a human being like an animal, we know deep down that it is terribly wrong. Whatever our failings (and the Bible shows us that each of us has many), we still image something of God, however incompletely and imperfectly.

This begins to show us the significance of sex. My friend and colleague Abdu Murray puts it this way:

> *Human sacredness leads us to see why human sexuality is sacred and worth protecting. When we fawn over a baby, we're not coldly observing a mere organism. We're beholding ... one who bears divine fingerprints. Sex between a man and a woman is the only means by which such a precious being comes into this world. And because a human being is the sacred product of sex, the sexual process by which that person is made is also sacred.*[14]

---

14 Abdu Murray, *Saving Truth* (Zondervan), p 137.

Given the unique value of human life, the creation of a new human life is bound to be deeply significant. If people are so precious, it won't surprise us if the means by which they're made also turns out to be precious.

In the United States new currency is produced by the Bureau of Engraving and Printing, part of the Department of the Treasury. Producing new currency is no small thing. The process is intricate and expensive. As well as the more obvious parts of the process like design and engraving, there are lesser-known specialisms like siderography, where various elements are combined into what we see on the front or back of a bank note. The single biggest piece of equipment in the whole process is the Large Examining Printing Equipment machine. These are each 144 feet long (44m—nearly half the length of an American football field), and contain 20 cameras which perform various verifications and inspections. Needless to say, this technology, and the process that it's part of, is not cheap. The 2019 budget for producing currency and coin in the USA was $955.8 million.

This should not surprise us. Money is—obviously—valuable. The process by which it is produced was therefore never going to be cheap.

If human life is sacred to God, then the process by which new human life is produced is also going to be sacred. That's how significant we human beings are. God cares about sex precisely because he cares about us. It matters, because we do. How could it be otherwise? It would be hard to imagine a God who regards each human life as precious being indifferent to the process by which that human life is made.

And that process is necessary for the task God gives people to do in the account of creation.

FILLING THE EARTH

The first purpose the Bible describes for sex is procreation:

> *God blessed them and said to them, "Be fruitful and increase in number; fill the earth and subdue it. Rule over the fish in the sea and the birds in the sky and over every living creature that moves on the ground."*
>
> GENESIS 1 v 28

This command is not arbitrary. If people are made in his image, God wants his image to fill the earth—for the whole world to perfectly reflect who he is. His image-bearers are therefore told to reproduce his image so that it can be spread across the globe and God's presence and loving rule perfectly represented through his people.

In other words, sex was God's idea, not ours. It is not something we discovered behind God's back. Nor is it something he has only begrudgingly allowed to us do. His first command to humanity in the Bible involves and necessitates sex.

In our culture we tend to think of sex primarily (and in some cases exclusively) as being about *recreation*. It is simply meant to be a means of enjoyment, with no unchosen reproductive consequences. We see this sexual freedom more and more as a fundamental right, and any perceived obstacle to it as an existential threat. Uncomfortable though it may be, the Bible challenges this way of thinking. Sex is introduced in the context of reproduction. It is ordered toward the creation of new life. To attempt to fully uncouple it from this wider context and purpose is to misunderstand it, and even to misuse it.

This is not to say that sex is only about reproduction. For sure, in the Bible, it is not *only* re-creative, but nor is it *only* pro-creative. The second chapter in Genesis highlights this for us. Sex has another, distinct purpose.

CREATING "ONE-NESS"

The account of creation in Genesis is formed of two parts. We've touched on the first, which is a "wide-angle lens" view of creation. The second focuses in on the first human couple, Adam and Eve. We are given the account of their meeting and getting together:

> *The man said,*
> *"This is now bone of my bones and flesh of my flesh;*
> *she shall be called 'woman,'*
> *for she was taken out of man."*
>
> *That is why a man leaves his father and mother and is united to his wife, and they become one flesh.*
>
> *Adam and his wife were both naked, and they felt no shame.* Genesis 2 v 23-24

Adam celebrates the creation of Eve. He immediately recognises that she is made of the same "stuff" as him—unlike the animals which have been his only company up to this point. She is unique. Made from him and like him in a way that is true of nothing else. They belong together. They were literally made for each other. So we're not surprised to see them get together.

This is significant. That the Bible opens with this as its first scene of human interaction shows us it must be important. The outcome of this scene shows us why: the two have become "one flesh." In other words, sex is part of the process by which the two become one. It is intended to have a profoundly unifying effect on two people.

This is what gives sex such power. And like any powerful force, it needs to be used rightly, which means being used in the right setting. It is helpful to think of sex as if it were fire.

Right now, I'm writing this in someone's living room, which is dominated by a large and ornate fireplace. This is the one place in the house where we can light a fire. Light one here and it gives light, warmth and life. Light one anywhere else and it will be dangerous, destructive and even life-threatening. In the right place it can perfectly enhance a home. In the wrong place it can burn the whole thing to the ground.

Sex is like that. It is a form of "holy fire".[15] In the right context it expresses and deepens a particular form of love. In the wrong context it can cause enormous pain and destruction. This is why the Bible insists on sex only being for a particular setting. Within this, sex can be a gift from God. Outside the right context, it can become harmful.

There is no easy way around this. From start to finish, the Bible speaks of sex as the one-flesh union of a man and a woman, designed and intended for the context of marriage. Even writing these lines, I feel how deeply offensive it sounds in this day and age. It may feel arbitrary—perhaps even harmful to you—to restrict sex in this way. But if you are able to carry on reading, please stick around long enough to see *why* the Bible teaches this, however difficult it may sound to you now. Believe it or not, Christians understand this framework for sex to be the outworking of a deeply positive message about the meaning of male and female, and of our need for deep connection as human beings.

All this comes from unpacking that tiny, innocuous-looking phrase "one flesh". It describes more than simply a bond of adult love that could exist irrespective of the gender or number of people involved. In the Bible, "one flesh" is actually telling us a story—a story that involves all of us. It both sets the God-given boundary for sex and points to its glory.

---

15   I'm grateful to Glen Scrivener for this phrase.

SEX AND (RE)CONNECTION

In the account of the creation of Eve, we read that God puts Adam into a deep sleep, removes a rib, and then forms Eve out of that rib (Genesis 2 v 21-22). Adam acknowledges this in his initial response to her: "She was taken out of man". When they then come together in sexual union, it is a rejoining of flesh that had been separated in her creation. Their uniting is a reuniting of sorts.

Writer Ronald Rolheiser finds evidence of this even in the word *sex*:

> *The word sex has a Latin root, the verb secare. In Latin, secare means (literally) "to cut off," "to sever," "to amputate," "to disconnect from the whole."*

Slightly disturbing, but he continues to this powerful conclusion:

> *Long before we even come to self-consciousness and long before we reach puberty when our sexuality con-stellates so strongly around the desire for sex, we feel ourselves painfully sexed in every cell of our body, psyche, and soul... We wake up in the world and in every cell of our being we ache, consciously and un-consciously, sensing that we are incomplete, unwhole, lonely, cut off, a little piece of something that was once part of a whole.*[16]

In other words, our longing for completeness is not about physical, sexual fulfilment, as though that would in itself make us feel full and whole. Instead, our sexual desires are but one particularly acute reflection of a much deeper desire

---

16 Ronald Rolheiser, *The Holy Longing: The Search for a Christian Spirituality* (New York: Image, 1998, 2014), p 193-194.

all of us have to be whole. The reunion of Adam and Eve is a picture of that fuller wholeness we all so deeply seek.

SEX AND THE INTERDEPENDENCE OF THE SEXES

Genesis 1 – 2 also tells us something important about the relationship between male and female:

> *So God created mankind in his own image,*
> *in the image of God he created them;*
> *male and female he created them.*
>
> GENESIS 1 v 26-27

Our being made as male and female is bound up with our being made in God's image. Human beings are obviously not the only creatures to be made male and female. I am in a house with a male dog, a male cat and two female cats. But we humans are the only creatures where this sexual differentiation carries this kind of significance: these verses in Genesis 1 show us that *we need each other* as men and women to better image God. It is not that men and women each constitute half of God's image and need the other to complete it. No, each is already made in the image of God. But there is something in the interplay between the two sexes that helps all of us together to image God more fully.

Consider the following thought experiment. Imagine a town or city exclusively populated by men, for example. Many of us would suspect that a community like this would become dysfunctional in a variety of ways. We sense that each sex is able to moderate something of the other sex and add something to it. We *need* each other. The interplay between the two is mutually enriching.

This is true on any level of interaction, but it reaches its highest form within marriage. The two become *one flesh*.

Writer Tim Keller puts it like this:

> *Male and female have unique, non-interchangeable glories—they each see and do things that the other cannot. Sex was created by God to be a way to mingle these strengths and glories within a life-long covenant of marriage. Marriage is the most intense (though not the only) place where this reunion of male and female takes place in human life. Male and female reshape, learn from, and work together.*[17]

The language of Genesis 2 reinforces this and leads us to our next observation.

SEX AND UNITY IN DIFFERENCE

The man and the woman, we're told, become "one flesh". The Hebrew word for "one" is *'echad*, and isn't about numerical value but about *unity*—something being of a single, whole piece. The oneness is a sense of integration and wholeness.

The same Hebrew word is used in Deuteronomy 6:4 to say one of the most foundational things about God in the Old Testament: "Hear, O Israel: The LORD our God, the LORD is One". It's not just saying there's only one God—though that itself is a significant claim the Bible makes—but that the one God who is there is a deep and profound unity.

In the Genesis 1 account of God creating humanity God speaks of himself as an "us": "let *us* make ... in *our* image" (Genesis 1 v 26). This hints at there being a plurality to God, and yet he is One.

17 Tim Keller, "The Bible and Same Sex Relationships: A Review Article" *Redeemer Report*, June 2015, www.bit.ly/occasleep7 (accessed 21 August 2019).

The New Testament goes on to describe God as being Father, Son and Holy Spirit—three distinct but united Persons—and so this unity is actually a *triunity* (which is where the Christian understanding of God being Trinity comes from). The three are distinct. They are not interchangeable. But they are one.

It is something of this unity we see reflected in the union between Adam and Eve. They are one in a way that reflects or images how God is one. It is not unity in sameness or in uniformity but in difference.

This goes some way to accounting for why the Bible presents marriage as being only between a man and a woman. Keller goes on:

> *In one of the great ironies of late modern times, when we celebrate diversity in so many other cultural sectors, we have truncated the ultimate unity-in-diversity: inter-gendered marriage.*

In our culture today, we tend to think of marriage primarily as an opportunity to celebrate deeply fulfilling romantic feelings adult people have for one another. If this is the primary focus, then it doesn't really make any difference if the people involved are men or women. Nor does it matter if there are just two people involved. We are seeing increasing calls for "throuples" to be able to legally marry, and even for people to be able to marry themselves in what is being called "sologamy".[18] If marriage is primarily about mutual romantic fulfilment, this all makes sense, and it would seem deeply unfair to exclude certain types of relationship from being able to get married.

---

18 BBC news. www.bit.ly/occasleep8 (accessed 21 August 2019).

The writer Andrew Sullivan, who is himself gay, puts it like this:

> *From being a means to bringing up children, it has become primarily a way in which two adults affirm their emotional commitment to one another.*[19]

But the account in Genesis 2 suggests there is more than romantic fulfilment behind the meaning of marriage. The one-flesh union is not the crescendo of romantic fulfilment; it is the highest form of unity between and man and a woman.

The biological complementarity of male and female is such that the physical and sexual union of a man and a woman is unlike any other. The union itself is unique. And so we should expect it to have a unique meaning and purpose for us, which brings us to the purpose of marriage.

19 Andrew Sullivan, *Same-Sex Marriage: Pro and Con: A Reader* (New York: Vintage, 1997, 2004), p.xxiii.

Is sex really just for marriage?

Sometimes a gift isn't quite as generous as it seems. It looks expensive and high-quality but turns out to be an imitation. Or it's actually faulty. Or it was a re-gift that they didn't want any more. Whatever the reason, what looked really generous turns out to be a little cheaper than we thought.

Something of this happens when we try to take sex out of the context for which it was designed. Because of how pleasurable sex can be, we tend to think of it in the way we think of other pleasurable things: *how we can make the most of it?* When we scan a menu, we think, "What will be tastiest? What do I fancy right now?" And with sex we can instinctively think, "What would satisfy me the most?"

This is a natural way to think. But if this is all that dominates our minds, we risk missing something that's right at the heart of what sex is for: *giving*.

We've already seen that the Bible is not anti-sex, and now we begin to see why. One author sums up the Bible's perspective on the purpose of sex like this:

> *Sex is God's appointed way for two people to reciprocal-*
> *ly say to one another, "I belong completely, permanent-*
> *ly, and exclusively to you."* [20]

If this is so, it has beautiful and radical implications for our attitude to sex. To reduce sex to being a means of getting pleasure is actually to hold back from someone what is meant to be a complete, permanent and exclusive form of self-giving. We might think we're giving someone the gift of a sexual relationship, but if we're not giving our whole self to them fully, then our gift turns out to be a lot cheaper than it first appeared.

That's a big claim to make, so we need to take a step back and see both *how* and *why* it is that the Bible arrives at this conclusion.

When we think about the teaching of Jesus, it comes into clearer focus:

> *Some Pharisees came to him to test him. They asked,*
> *"Is it lawful for a man to divorce his wife for any and*
> *every reason?"*
>
> *"Haven't you read," he replied, "that at the beginning*
> *the Creator 'made them male and female,' and said,*
> *'For this reason a man will leave his father and mother*
> *and be united to his wife, and the two will become*
> *one flesh'? So they are no longer two, but one flesh.*
> *Therefore what God has joined together, let no one*
> *separate."*
>
> MATTHEW 19 v 3-6

---

20 Tim Keller, *The Meaning of Marriage*, (Dutton, 2011), p 224.

Notice the connection Jesus makes between Genesis 1 v 27 (which he quotes in the first paragraph) and Genesis 2 v 24 (which he quotes in second). Jesus is asked about divorce but answers by pointing to the one-flesh union in marriage. But if one-flesh union existed in any kind of sexual union, irrespective of the sex of those involved, he would not have needed to say more than this. But he does. He reaches back, not just to Genesis 2 but to Genesis 1, and reiterates that God has created humanity as male and female.

It is this which explains the one-flesh union of a man and a woman. God has sexually differentiated us as male and female, and this differentiation is foundational to who we are as image-bearers. Other significant differences exist between us, and the interplay between those differences is also enriching. But none of those other differences are as defining in the Bible as the difference between male and female. Genesis 1 does not say that "God created them introvert and extrovert" or "left-brain and right-brain" or even "black and white." The sexual difference is what is defining, and therefore it is the union between male and female that has uniquely enriching potential for us, and which alone can enable two people to become one flesh.

There is a huge amount to say on all this. It raises important and understandable questions about sexuality and gender identity which are beyond our scope here.[21] What is essential to understand is how the interplay between male and female is foundational to the Christian understanding of sexual ethics.

---

21 For more on these important questions, see Sam Allberry, *Is God Anti-Gay?* (The Good Book Company, 2013), and Andrew Walker, *God and the Transgender Debate* (The Good Book Company, 2017).

SEX AS A MEANS OF SELF-GIVING

The apostle Paul writes these instructions to the church in Corinth:

> *The husband should fulfil his marital duty to his wife, and likewise the wife to her husband. The wife does not have authority over her own body but yields it to her husband. In the same way, the husband does not have authority over his own body but yields it to his wife.*
>
> 1 CORINTHIANS 7 v 3-4

We'll come to how revolutionary this would have sounded to the ancient world in the next chapter, but for now notice how Paul counsels *both* husband and wife to be self-giving in their sex life. This sense of deep mutual belonging is also prominent in the Old Testament book *Song of Songs*, a book celebrating the love between a young man and woman. "I am my beloved's and my beloved is mine," says the young bride (Song of Songs 6 v 3). Sex is designed to be a form of giving oneself completely to the other, hence Paul's teaching to husbands and wives: the body of each belongs to the other. This is what sex is designed to be.

Even within this mutuality, Paul's focus is on the other person. Paul speaks of sexually serving the other. He doesn't write that each partner is to *take* their marital rights from the other, but that each is to *give* to the other what is *their* right. The focus is on serving and pleasing the other. Elsewhere, speaking to a group of pastors, Paul could recall…

> *…the words of the Lord Jesus Christ, how he himself said, "It is more blessed to give than to receive".*
>
> ACTS 20 v 35

Clearly this applies to the marriage bed as much as to church ministry. Husband and wife are to be focused on the sexual satisfaction of the other person, not on themselves. Sex is not a commodity to be transacted but a means of devotion to the other.

So the Christian view of how we should think about sex could be summarised as follows. Each partner in a marriage should be more concerned about *giving* pleasure, not getting it. In short, the greatest sexual pleasure to be experienced should be the pleasure of seeing your spouse getting pleasure.

Having made his point in the positive, Paul goes on to make it in the negative:

> *Do not deprive each other, except perhaps by mutual consent and for a time, so that you may devote yourselves to prayer. Then come together again so that Satan may not tempt you because of your lack of self-control.* 1 CORINTHIANS 7 v 5

Fulfilling your "marital duty" to your spouse is so important that Paul forbids couples from depriving one another, and he can only envisage them doing so temporarily, by consent, and for a season of prayer. Beyond that, the couple are in spiritual danger. It is worth noting that, according to Paul, the only person who is against sex in this context is Satan!

SEX AS A MEANS OF GIVING THE ENTIRE SELF

It is also clear that this one-flesh union involves more than sex. What this "one flesh" is and means indicates that it is not just about what has happened to two bodies but to the totality of who each person is. It is not just that our bodies are involved with each other's in sex; our entire personhood is involved. Jesus himself alludes to this in a passage where he quotes these words from Genesis 2:

> *"Haven't you read,"* he replied, *"that at the beginning the Creator 'made them male and female,' and said, 'For this reason a man will leave his father and mother and be united to his wife, and the two will become one flesh'? So they are no longer two, but one flesh. Therefore what God has joined together, let no one separate."*
> MATTHEW 19 v 4-6

Jesus speaks of this union as being made *by God*—in some sense *he* has joined the two people together. That he says they must not be separated shows that there is a degree of union that remains after a couple has had sex. They might not be physically joined any more, but at a deeper level they are still united.

This is hugely important. Sexual union is both an expression of and vehicle for a wider and deeper form of union, and this greater union is not designed to be undone. Sex is a means by which two people are being united not just physically but also emotionally and psychologically. Our culture often claims that we can give someone our physical body without giving them our whole self, but Christians would say that this is not so.

The apostle Paul shows us why this is:

> *Flee from sexual immorality. All other sins a person commits are outside the body, but whoever sins sexually sins against his own body.*
> 1 CORINTHIANS 6 v 18

Notice what Paul is saying about sex. What we do sexually affects the whole body in a way that is not generally true of other things. Whether we know it or not, or mean it or not, Paul is saying that sex engages far more of who we are than merely our genitals. It involves the whole person.

This is a positive truth about sex, but it is perhaps tragically seen most clearly in the negative. When someone is wronged sexually, it is more than just a couple of parts of the body that are affected. One thing is very clear: the whole person is impacted. The damage is not just physical, but emotional and psychological too. These wounds can last a lifetime and manifest themselves in a thousand different ways. Sex is not just about parts of our biology. When someone is sexually assaulted or when someone is sexually betrayed, it is not just their body that is attacked—*they* as a person are violated.

This is the flipside of a good thing. Sex is meant to be about far more than a physical release. It is meant to *mean* something. That it involves the whole person indicates that two whole selves are meant to be engaging with each other. Hook-up culture is a denial of this, insisting that the sexual dimension can be expressed and satisfied independently of the other aspects of who we are. It is saying, in effect, that the other person is only worth the gift of some of who you actually are as a person.

YOUR BODY MAKES A PROMISE

In the 2001 movie *Vanilla Sky*, Tom Cruise's character has a one-night stand with a woman played by Cameron Diaz. Later on in the movie she challenges him on this. At one point she says, "Don't you know that when you sleep with someone, your body makes a promise whether you do or not?" In other words, what is going on with the body is meant to be a token of what is meant to be happening at a deeper level. We might say that to engage in the physical part of sexual intimacy with no thought for this deeper union is a form of deception.

As well as being the author of *The Chronicles of Narnia*, C.S. Lewis was a noted Christian thinker and writer. In perhaps his most celebrated book, *Mere Christianity*, Lewis says that sex apart from the context of this deeper union is an attempt "to isolate one kind of union (the sexual) from all the other kinds of union which were intended to go along with it and make up the total union". Tim Keller adds:

> *Every sex act is supposed to be a uniting act. Paul insists it is radically dissonant to give your body to someone to whom you will not commit your whole life.*

He continues,

> *If sex is a method that God invented to do "whole life entrustment" and self-giving, it should not surprise us that sex makes us feel deeply connected to the other person, even when used wrongly. Unless you deliberately disable it, or through practice you numb the original impulse, sex makes you feel personally interwoven and joined to another human being, as you are literally physically joined.*

If this is the case—that sex is fundamentally about giving, and about giving our whole self to someone—then having sex with someone without the intention of giving them this is actually a form of taking. It is theft.

ONE SCENE, TWO SCENARIOS

Perhaps a couple of (imperfect) analogies might help.

Imagine you're walking past a bank lobby, and you see someone standing at one of the service desks, and a teller is passing them a large wad of banknotes. There are two possible things that might be going on. It might be that the person is a customer of the bank and is making a legitimate (if large) withdrawal, and the cashier is simply handing over the money. Or it might be that the person is standing there with a gun and actually holding up the bank, and demanding the cashier give them money. In both cases the same physical act is taking place (handing the money over), but in the context of two very different narratives, and it is these narratives that determine the moral quality of the act.

Or think about when someone gives someone else a present for purely selfish reasons. A friend of mine recently admitted they had given their spouse a certain cooking implement simply because they wanted them to make the sort of food it was designed to cook. It looks, at first, like generosity—they're giving a gift to someone—but it is ultimately self-serving.

These two analogies reflect something of the difference between sex outside of marriage and sex within it. The act may seem to be the same in both cases, but the narrative of which it is part actually reveals whether it is morally just or not. The former might be justified as giving someone a gift—"I'm giving you my love"—but if they're holding back from whole-life self-giving, it's ultimately giving something that's really for themselves and not the other person.

The Bible teaches repeatedly that sexual intimacy is only appropriate within the covenant of marriage. Marriage is meant to be the means by which we promise to give ourselves to someone else fully and exclusively, vowing whole-life commitment to the other that sex is meant to be both an expression and means of.

We see this reflected in a number of Bible passages. Jesus himself teaches that sexual immorality is one of the evidences that our hearts are not as they should be:

> *For out of the heart come evil thoughts—murder, adul-*
> *tery, sexual immorality, theft, false testimony, slander.*
> *These are what defile a person.* MATTHEW 15 v 19-20

The phrase we translate "sexual immorality" is the Greek word *porneia*, a catch-all term for any sexual conduct outside the covenant of marriage. It would include sex before marriage, adultery (which Jesus mentions separately in this list), prostitution, and even same-sex sexual behaviour.

It is sometimes easy to think that sex before marriage and sex within marriage are essentially the same and that the only difference is timing—that sex before marriage vows and sex after marriage vows is no different. But this is not so. Sex outside of these vows is a different act to sex that is expressing and reinforcing these vows. One is establishing a context of lifelong self-giving; the other is a form of taking.

Sex, according to the Bible, is precious—more so than we tend to realise. Not because it is a means by which we can experience gratification. That can happen, of course (just read *Song of Songs*), but it is not the sole aim. The purpose is not what we can *get*, but what we can *give*. Let's conclude where we began, with the words of Tim Keller:

> *Sex is God's appointed way for two people to reciprocal-*
> *ly say to one another, "I belong completely, permanent-*
> *ly, and exclusively to you." We must not use sex to say*
> *anything else.*

God cares who we sleep with because of what he has designed sex to do. It is an extremely powerful force. It is meant to be. Needless to say, this raises all sorts of important questions: How can this be right if it is so counter-cultural? How is this even good for us? We'll attempt to address these in the next chapter.

Why was this so controversial back then?

There's an app for that.

I recently downloaded an app that orders home delivery from a range of local restaurants. I was away from home in a new city, and having been teaching all day, I was feeling tired, hungry and somewhat emotionally drained. I didn't have the means to cook, there wasn't a restaurant at the hotel, and I didn't feel like I had the energy to go somewhere and have to interact with people. So I downloaded the app.

It listed a range of local eateries from which a meal could be delivered to me and, a few flicks of the thumb later, a serving of pasta and meatballs was on its way. Not a cheap way to procure food—the mark-up is quite significant—but it was certainly the easiest.

The parallels with how we often think about sex are striking. Again, we might find ourselves feeling tired and drained and yet with a keen hunger for sexual satisfaction. We might be somewhere where we don't know people—where perhaps our normal means for satisfying that hunger are not available.

So we turn to an app. On it, local available options are presented to us. All that it takes is a couple of swipes of the thumb, and in a matter of minutes we can hook up with someone. Again, it is amazingly easy.

It is common to think of sex simply as a commodity, a matter of transaction, a means of satisfying a bodily appetite no more complicated than when we eat food to satisfy our hunger.

Drawing a parallel between food and sex was familiar to the Christians in Corinth. One of their slogans was "Food is for the stomach and the stomach for food" (their equivalent of a hashtag; see 1 Corinthians 6 v 13). It was used as a justification for sexual permissiveness. Their thinking was that just as you eat when you're hungry, you have sex when you're horny. It is just biological. What's the big deal? We don't make this kind of fuss about food; why should we make it about sex?

We've begun to see how the Bible answers these questions. Sex is not just biological. It is not just a bodily activity. It involves the whole of who we are.

And as we saw at the end of the previous chapter, this raises important questions: How can this Christian ethic be right if it is so countercultural? Surely it should be more intuitive to us. But instead it seems to go against the grain of how so many people naturally think today. And how can this ethic be good? It feels very constraining. Surely it is actually harmful to deprive someone of the sort of sex they want, just as it is harmful to legislate what sort of food people should be able to eat.

To begin to think about this, it can help to look at how countercultural Christian thinking about sex was in the culture in which it was first taught. The Corinthians were not atypical in thinking the way they did about matters of sexuality. Sexual norms in the Roman world were much the same as in Corinth. They were very different from our own. And they were even more different from those of the Christian faith.

COUNTERCULTURAL SEXUALITY IN THE ROMAN WORLD

New Testament scholar F.F. Bruce sums up in this way:

> *Christianity from the outset has sanctified sexual union within marriage (as in Judaism); outside marriage it was forbidden. This was a strange notion in the pagan society to which the gospel was first brought; there were various forms of extra-marital sexual union were tolerated and some were even encouraged. A man might have a mistress who could provide him also with intellectual companionship; the institution of slavery made it easy for him to have a concubine, while casual gratification was readily available from a harlot. The function of his wife was to manage the household and be the mother of his legitimate children and heirs. There was no body of public opinion to discourage [this], although someone who indulged in it to excess might be satirized on the same level as a notorious glutton or drunkard.*[22]

The pronouns in this are deliberate and telling. This was the situation for a *man* in the Roman world. *He* could have access to a mistress, concubine and/or prostitute. The same was not the case for women; they had significantly less sexual freedom.

Historian Kyle Harper has expanded on this; his book

---

22   F.F. Bruce, *1 and 2 Thessalonians* Word Biblical Commentary, (Word, 1982), p 82.

From Shame to Sin[23] demonstrates how closely linked sexual ethics and customs were to social standing in the ancient Roman world. Adultery was forbidden as shameful; not so much because it was a violation of a married woman but because it was seen as a violation of the man she was thought to be the property of—it was theft.[24] Sex with slaves was allowed instead, and if you couldn't afford slaves, the prostitute was "a safety valve for male lust".[25] Slavery and brothels were seen as a vital part of maintaining broader sexual propriety by keeping adultery in check.

In all this, women were at a significant disadvantage. Those who were faithfully married were given protection by Roman society. But prostitutes were seen as shameful. Their bodies were given no such protection and were regarded as available to men for sexual gratification. When it came to sex, women were a commodity. If they were regarded as honourable, then they were a prized commodity but a commodity nonetheless—if shameful, a cheap and available commodity for those seeking it. Their sexuality was not grounded in their personhood as women but in their place in society. Slaves and poor women were readily and often exploited.[26]

Male slaves could just as easily be abused, and very frequently were, due to their low status in society. Age, too, wasn't a factor in determining whether sex was appropriate. Boys and girls were also subject to sexual exploitation if they were slaves or prostitutes.

Against this backdrop, the sexual ethics introduced by the Christian faith were unprecedented. Harper has gone as far

---

23 Kyle Harper, *From Shame to Sin* (Harvard University Press, 2013).

24 *From Shame to Sin*, p 56.

25 *From Shame to Sin*, p 46-47.

26 *From Shame to Sin*, p 18.

as to call this "the first sexual revolution".[27] The teaching of the New Testament was profoundly countercultural in some massive ways.

1. Constraints on men

First, Scripture insists on sexual boundaries and controls for men and not just for women. If the shock to our contemporary ears is that *anyone* should be expected to be sexually restrained in some way, the shock to first-century people would have been that it was expected of *men*, even of free men of high standing. The whole system of sexual ethics was built around the notion that men had freedom to satisfy their sexual urges in any of the accepted ways.

In contrast to this, Paul instructs men to "avoid sexual immorality; that each of you should learn to control your own body in a way that is holy and honourable" (1 Thessalonians 4 v 3-4). This is a word to Christians in general, but expected of men no less than women. They are just as obligated to control their bodies and resist any kind of sexual sin.

In the New Testament, "sexual immorality" includes far more than merely violating Roman codes of sexual conduct. As with the consistent teaching of the Old Testament, the New Testament teaches that any kind of sex outside the covenant of marriage is prohibited. Christian men, therefore, were not permitted to sleep with prostitutes or slaves of either sex, any more than they were permitted to sleep with the wife of another free man. Christian sexual ethics were not determined by a person's status and social value in Roman society but by the unique and complementary dignity of men and women as God's image-bearers.

---

27   Kyle Harper, "The First Sexual Revolution: How Christianity Transformed the Ancient World", *First Things*, January 2018.

Christian men, in contrast to their secular counterparts, were to be exclusively faithful to their wives. For many typical Roman men, this would have been unthinkable and even humiliating. If they were men of high social standing, that meant they had certain sexual freedoms. But according to the Christian faith, your position in society has no bearing on your obligation to abide by the sexual ethics that come with the gospel of Jesus.

2. Mutuality

Secondly, the Christian faith brought with it a radical mutuality in its understanding of sex within marriage. As we've seen, there was a huge imbalance between the sexual freedoms and rights of men and women in the Roman world. Men had the power. Women, if they were fortunate, had the protection of social standing, but other than that they were frequently at the mercy of men more wealthy and powerful than they were. Even within marriage, the role of the wife was primarily to provide legitimate heirs. For deeper sexual satisfaction the husbands could turn elsewhere.

Consider these words of the apostle Paul, and we can begin to see how revolutionary his teaching would have sounded:

> *Each man should have sexual relations with his own wife, and each woman with her own husband. The husband should fulfil his marital duty to his wife, and likewise the wife to her husband. The wife does not have authority over her own body but yields it to her husband. In the same way, the husband does not have authority over his own body but yields it to his wife.*
> 1 Corinthians 7 v 2-4

We briefly looked at these words at the end of the previous chapter. It is hard to overstate how radical this would have been at the time it was first written.

The first part of what Paul says here would have sounded very familiar: each woman should have sex with her husband, should fulfil her marital duty, and does not have authority over her own body but gives it to her husband. This was all assumed. It was the normal way to think.

But the unprecedented step Paul takes is making this entirely *mutual*. The husband physically belongs to his wife *just as much* as she physically belongs to him. He should be fulfilling his marital duty to her *just as much* as she should be fulfilling hers to him. In other words, it is not simply the case that a wife has responsibilities to her husband; *he* has the very same responsibilities to *her*. Both parties are equal. Each is to be served by the other. This was unheard of.

But though this would have been a new idea to the Roman world, it was not a new idea to the Bible. The Old Testament love poem, the Song of Songs, includes this mutuality throughout the refrain, "My beloved is mine, and I am his" (Song of Songs 2 v 16); "I am my beloved's and my beloved is mine" (6 v 3). The biblical vision for sexual intimacy has always included this idea of reciprocity. The goal is not simply the gratification of the more powerful partner.

3. Consent

This mutuality is the basis for a third significant distinctive in the Christian vision for sex: *consent*—perhaps the most important sexual ethic Western society continues to insist upon. Paul would only countenance couples abstaining from sex by mutual consent, and the same is true of having sex too. Paul understood that both parties in the marriage have what Harper calls "complete sexual agency." Theologian Beth Felkner Jones underlines the significance of this:

We've already seen that sex as commodity was a pillar of the Roman Empire. Christian sexual ethics developed as a rebuke of that world. Christians claimed that Christ gave us the kind of freedom that allows us to choose sexual holiness. Truly consensual sex was a rarity in the world in which Christianity got its start. Christianity, we might say, invented consensual sex.[28]

And not just consent about having sex, but even about whether or not to get married. That word "even" sounds superfluous to us because the choice to get married is such a given in western culture. But that is because our culture has been so heavily influenced by the Christian faith. Paul writes to the Corinthians that a woman can *choose* to be married or to be single (1 Corinthians 7 v 6-9). Paul commends singleness as being of some advantage in some ways (v 35), but he recognises that there is freedom for the believer as to whether they remain single or marry. Each is a gift from God (v 7). Here is Jones again:

Roman women were not free not to marry. Christian women could choose—even insist on—celibacy. For Christians, women aren't property or baby makers ... Men aren't lust machines or power mongers.[29]

Jones sums up the principle differences between Roman and Christian ideas about sex as follows:

In Rome, some people (potential wives, for instance) got protection and honor, and some did not. In the kingdom

28 Beth Felker Jones, *Faithful* (Zondervan, 2015), p 80 (emphasis mine).

29 *Faithful*, p 97.

[i.e. the kingdom of God], everybody's body is honored. In Rome, bodies were for power or pleasure or the state or the market. In the kingdom, we are all called to be chaste, all of our bodies are not for [sexual sin] but for the Lord. In Rome, if you were sexually shameful, there was no going back. In God's kingdom, there is forgiveness and healing and grace and freedom.[30]

Christian sexual ethics have been countercultural in every culture. This is important to understand. It is easy to assume that Christian sexual ethics are old-fashioned. But that presumes some prior time in history when the Bible's teaching neatly matched our own sensibilities. But this has never been the case.

There *have* been times when particular cultures have been significantly influenced by Christianity in this regard, but the teaching of the Bible always ends up critiquing major aspects of any culture's view of sex and marriage, even while affirming other aspects. We might look at the Bible's teaching in horror, exclaiming, *But it's the Twenty-First Century!* But it's not all that different from someone in the Roman Empire reading Paul's letter to the Thessalonians for the first time, exclaiming *But this is the First Century!* Though the reasons have varied from age to age and culture to culture, Christian teaching on this issue has never been in vogue.

---

30 *Faithful*, p 72.

Why is this so controversial today?

We can see the ways the Christian view of sex was revolutionary in the Roman world into which it was first introduced. But the same is true today. We are not Rome, and we look back on many of their practices with dismay and even revulsion. Yet there is much the Christian sexual ethic challenges us on in our own day. Just as we might now be able to see how the Bible's teaching was good for the Roman Empire, we might now be able to start considering how that same teaching is good for us in our own culture.

We tend to think very casually about lust. The idea of desiring another person sexually doesn't tend to concern us today (unless the person in question is a child). What we think about in the privacy of our own mind is our own business. It doesn't affect anyone else, and it doesn't really affect us. It is, we often assume, a healthy part of human sexuality.

We have already seen how Jesus counters this way of thinking.

> You have heard that it was said, "You shall not commit adultery". But I tell you that anyone who looks at a

woman lustfully has already committed adultery with
her in his heart. MATTHEW 5 v 27-28

Jesus says even looking and thinking lustfully is not right. It is not good for us, and it is not good for the other person. We may think it is entirely harmless, but Jesus begs to differ.

So why is this so serious?

According to Jesus, there is more going on than we might realise. Something very significant is going on when we lust. We are actually shaping how we view the world around us. One of the later Ten Commandments shows us how:

You shall not covet your neighbour's house. You shall
not covet your neighbour's wife, or his male or female
servant, his ox or donkey, or anything that belongs to
your neighbour. EXODUS 20 v 17

This is the last of the Ten Commandments, and it prohibits coveting, which is wanting to have what belongs to someone else. The first thing to strike many contemporary readers is (to us) the bizarre way this commandment is then explained. Coveting an ox or donkey is probably not something you expected to be thinking about today, but for people then, these were important animals for travel and labour. It would be like us coveting the car in the driveway next door to us, or a neighbour's top-of-the-range device or appliance. The passage also mentions domestic staff, and again we can see the equivalent today: maybe envying someone being able to afford a cleaner or personal trainer.

But it also speaks about coveting someone's *wife*: not a possession or an object, or even an employee, but someone's spouse. In other words, the issue here is *greed*, and greed applies as much to people as it does to stuff. And the same greed that makes us wish we could get our hands on a friend's brand-new Lexus or iPhone can also make us wish we could get our hands on their partner too. To covet someone's spouse is to want to *possess* that person. It is treating them not as a person in their own right but as something to *have*.

This is what Jesus is getting at. Looking at someone with lustful intent is looking at someone purely as a means of gratification for you—as a means of satisfying a desire you have. It is turning them into a commodity to be consumed, rather than a person to honour. It makes their sexuality something for us to be satiated by.

YOU SAW HER BATHING ON THE ROOF...

We have already thought a little bit about King David sleeping with Bathsheba and some of the disastrous consequences. It is a sobering illustration of what sexual sin can lead to. But it is also an important commentary on what Jesus says about lust. Let's look at how these awful events actually unfolded.

In the account, David is on the roof of the royal palace when he happens to see a beautiful woman bathing. Once he determines who she is, he has her brought to him and he sleeps with her. This is often portrayed as a sordid affair, which would be bad enough given Bathsheba is married to a member of David's army who is at that very moment fighting in one of his wars. But it is far worse even than that.

David is the king, and she is a subject. There is an enormous power differential here; and no indication in the text that her consent was a factor. We are simply told that "David sent messengers and took her, and she came to him, and he lay with her" (2 Samuel 11 v 4). Royal officers arrive at her home and take her to the king, who then sleeps with her.

Things then start to spiral out of David's control. Bathsheba becomes pregnant. There's a botched attempt to get her husband back home for a conjugal visit so that the child can be passed off as theirs, but when that fails, David arranges to have her husband killed in battle and takes Bathsheba and the child into his palace. She loses her sexual integrity, her husband, and the life she once had. David takes it all.

Episodes like this remind us that for all the cultural and historical differences, the Bible deals with the very same world as our own. Characters are just as complex and flawed. There is the same sorry mess of brokenness and wickedness that we see all around us today.

A LUSTFUL LOOK

But notice how all of this—the whole sorry saga—began with a lustful look. That's all it took.

David was idling about on his rooftop. He saw Bathsheba bathing. However it began, he lingered over the image. What he was looking at was a person, a woman, a wife. What he made her with his eyes was a possession to be taken. She was evidently beautiful, but her beauty led David to covet her. It was something David felt he had a right to. Because *he* found her attractive, it was now fair game for him to use her looks to give him gratification. She was no longer a person but a commodity. He was dehumanising her. Her body was not her own property but his playground. And because he was the king, he had the power to then physically act on that with her, leading to the whole sorry chain of events that would leave her widowed, pregnant and forced into a new unchosen marriage.

But it never would have happened in actuality if it hadn't happened first in his attitude. He committed adultery with her in his heart before he physically committed adultery in his bedroom. Bathsheba, her husband, and the life she had known were all sacrificed to his lust.

This is what lust does. It reduces how we see others, and in the process dehumanises us. We become those who see less and less of the humanity in others. So it makes no difference if the objects of our lust are even aware of it. David's lust for Bathsheba would have been destructive to him even if he had never been able to physically act on it with her. It harms us before it harms anyone else.

Porn is a tragic example of this. It is well established that there is a direct connection between the consumption of online pornography and human trafficking. In the west we often look back on the abolition of the slave trade as a defining moment in our progress as a civilisation. We wonder how it could have taken so long to happen. We now look at once-revered slave-owning historical figures in a different, more critical way. We take down their statues and petition institutions named after them to be renamed. And yet we turn a blind eye to slavery when it is driven by lust.

Justin Holcomb writes:

> *Human trafficking is a form of modern-day slavery, and it's the fastest-growing criminal industry in the world. Sex trafficking is one of the most profitable forms of trafficking and involves many kinds of sexual exploitation, such as prostitution, pornography, bride trafficking, and the commercial sexual abuse of children. According to the United Nations, sex trafficking brings in an estimated $32 billion a year worldwide. In the United States, sex trafficking brings in $9.5 billion annually …*
>
> *The primary way porn fuels the sex trade is by building the demand. After all, the sex trade consists of supply and demand. The supply is women and children either*

forced into exploitation at home or lured away from their homes with promises of jobs, travel and a better life. The average age of girls who enter street prostitution is between 12 and 14—even younger in some developing countries. Traffickers coerce women and children through a variety of recruitment techniques to enter the commercial sex industry in strip clubs, street-based prostitution and escort services. Thousands of children and women are victimized in this way each year.[31]

It is not unusual for someone to be engaging in activism against human trafficking while at the same time accessing the online pornography that fuels so much of that very trafficking. Lust dehumanises both parties: the person seen from David's rooftop, or on our screens, is not a human being made in the image of God; they're a sexual commodity. We lose something of our normal human sensibility, becoming indifferent and desensitised to things which in our better moments we care deeply about. Jesus' teaching against looking lustfully is a protection not just for the person being looked at but for the person doing the looking. Lusting after someone, even in the privacy of our own mind and without their knowledge, eventually harms all concerned.

The message of Jesus, therefore, is controversial today because it *needs* to be. The moral inconsistencies and blindspots of the Roman Empire are now all too apparent to us. And yet we today have our own equivalents, and the teaching of the Bible helps us to see them more clearly.

At the same time, it is perhaps becoming apparent that this teaching exposes failings not just in our culture but in our own hearts. If what Jesus and the New Testament teach

---

31   Justin Holcomb, "Porn Is Not Harmless. It's Cruel" www.bit.ly/occasleep9 (accessed 27 August 2019).

is right—if this is what God indeed thinks about sex—it leaves us all very much having fallen short of his ways. There is not one of us who is not broken, warped and harmful to others in our sexuality. This is the uncomfortable implication of the message of Christianity. It puts us all in the same boat, but it's not a boat we'd want to find ourselves in.

So we need to come back to an ancient word used to describe the original message of Jesus. When Mark began his account of the life and ministry of Jesus, he did so in this way:

> *The beginning of the good news about Jesus the*
> *Messiah, the Son of God.*　　　　　　MARK 1 v 1

"Good news" here translates the Greek word that is also translated as *gospel*. It was the word people used at the time for positive dramatic announcements, like the birth of a child to Caesar, or victory for the empire against a far-flung foe. But Mark used it of Jesus. Jesus is good news—not just *some* good news but *the* good news.

The reason for this is that Jesus is not just good in the ethical standards he brings to us, much as we need them. He is good even in how he responds to us when we break those standards. God cares who we sleep with because he really does care about us, even when we fail, as all of us have. The message of Jesus to those who realise this could not be better, as David himself discovered a thousand years before. *Read on!*

What if I've really messed up?

One of the slightly obscure words that has come into the English language as a result of the teaching of Jesus is *beatitude*. It means "to be blessed", and the Beatitudes are a set of statements Jesus made that describe the sort of people God blesses—those he showers his favour and gifts on.

Here are the first couple, and they catch us off guard:

> *Blessed are the poor in spirit,*
> *for theirs is the kingdom of heaven.*
>
> *Blessed are those who mourn,*
> *for they will be comforted.*   Matthew 5 v 3-4

To be "poor in spirit" is to be someone who recognises they're not as spiritually great as they might have thought. To mourn, here particularly, includes the idea of grieving the ways in which we've not been the people we're meant to be.

Many of us will reach this chapter feeling a significant sense of regret. It might be the sort of buried regret we *really* don't want to think about. Or it might be the sort of very raw regret that we can't help thinking about. Some of us might not feel *any* regrets, but perhaps we should. Sexuality, as we've seen, is such a personal part of human life, and therefore it can affect us very deeply in different ways.

The Christian message confronts us. There's no way to avoid that, and I don't want to apologise for it. It confronts me too. And none of us like to be told that we've messed up far more than we might realise.

But the Christian message also lifts us up. God loves us far more than we dared hope, and what Jesus does for us as we live with bitter regrets, is to draw near to us and bless us.

So the Christian message is going to first confront us, and then lift us up, because it's going to say that we've messed up more than we realise, but also that we can be given a fresh start and a new hope that's more powerful than we might have dared hope.

The Bible's account of what we are all like may surprise you. We may be used to the idea of "sin", particularly in a religious context. But it is easy to misunderstand what this word really means for Christians. We often trivialise the concept (I'm thinking of an ice-cream brand that categorises calories as "sins") or else we minimise it, regarding only certain acts as being truly sinful and wrong.

But the message of Christianity sees sin as much more serious and much deeper. Sin is not just breaking rules; it is the twisting of our hearts. It is more to do with attitude than action. We've already seen this with Jesus' teaching on adultery and lust. But the fact is that our hearts are twisted in such a way that we can even do morally right things in a sinfully wrong way. If sin is the deep-down disposition of our hearts, then it means every area of life is tainted in some way by this.

CRUMBLED DESIRES

Think of it this way. My favourite dessert is what we Brits call apple crumble—stewed apples with a flour or oat-based crumble on top. A while ago I had Sunday lunch with some friends, and they announced that they'd made apple crumble especially for my visit. My glee at this was immediately offset when they then said they'd done "a bit of an experiment with it". I tried to smile politely but could only feel a sense of doom inside. Justifiably, it turns out.

I'm not sure what they'd added to it (based on the flavour, possibly plutonium), but it was horrible. And it didn't matter which part of it I took a spoonful from—top or bottom, this end of the dish or that—it all tasted awful. Whatever they'd put in it affected (and completely ruined) the whole thing.

This is what Christians believe sin is like. Our twisted hearts taint every single part of life. Whatever area of life you might happen to think about, none of us are everything we should be. It's not to say that every part of life is as bad as it could be; just that no part is as good as it should be.

So when the Bible talks about sexual sin, it is not singling sex out as being unique or worse than anything else. It is just being realistic about the fact that the peculiar skewing of the human heart will show itself in this area of life just as much as any other.

This being so, the answer to any kind of sin is not just behaviour modification. If the problem is what our hearts are like, then trying to conform to certain external ethical standards—rules—is not going to ultimately help us. It would be like trying to improve the symptoms without addressing the underlying issue. We don't need better behaviour; first and foremost we need new hearts.

This is so important when it comes to thinking about sexual behaviour. There are a couple of mistakes Christians often make here.

MISTAKES AND REMEDIES

One is to think that only certain other people are sexual sinners. We can do this if we look at external behaviour (and even then we tend not to know the half of what is really going on in someone's life). But Jesus has already shown us that the real issue is what goes on *in our hearts*, not just *our actions*. By his definition, we are all sinful and broken in this area of life. We might be that in very different ways, and even to different extents (though again we are not always best placed to determine such things), but none of us is in a position to be smug or self-righteous.

A second, related mistake is to put all the focus on improving people's sexual conduct: to lay down rules designed to restrict the opportunity for sexual sin. Trying to reduce the opportunity for sin is no bad thing, but on its own it massively misses the point: *the issue is our hearts*. Removing opportunities to sexually sin with our bodies is not going to make our hearts any better. Encouraging young Christians to make resolutions and pledges will do nothing if there is not a change of heart. It can also make someone believe, as and when they break one of these resolutions—which is not unlikely if the underlying issue of the heart is unaddressed—that they have "failed" Christianity and that there's no going back.

Thankfully the Bible doesn't just show us that we're all broken when it comes to sexuality; it shows us how to respond to that in a healthy way. One of the best examples of this is, once again, King David.

We've already seen the horrific mess David made, and the brutal way he treated Bathsheba and her family. It was one act of wickedness after another—lust leading to exploitation leading to deceit leading to murder and cover-up. Sometimes we feel that we have to sin our way out of the consequences of sin—by lying or hiding the truth—and it all snowballs into an unimaginable disaster.

Lots of things about David's situation were unique—he was a king and had unusual power to abuse and sin in the way he did. But he is also a picture of us all. We are all sexual sinners. We cannot develop sexually without sin tainting our sexuality in some way. It is very much true of me. If I was to be completely honest with you about some of the thoughts that have passed through my mind over the years, you would rightly be appalled. And it is also very much true of you. We should be conscious of this. It should concern us. It eventually came to concern David.

David was king, but a prophet was brave enough to challenge him about what had happened. David eventually came to terms with what he'd done, and he processed it before God in the form of a poetic prayer, which has since found its way into the Bible as Psalm 51. We might not have done all the things David did, but his response is very much a model for us to follow as we recognise the ways in which, in our sexuality, we are not the people we are meant to be either.

WHAT WE NEED TO DO

Look at the first couple of lines of David's Psalm:

> *Have mercy on me, O God,*
> *according to your unfailing love;*
> *according to your great compassion*
> *blot out my transgressions.*

Wash away all my iniquity
and cleanse me from my sin.   PSALM 51 v 1-2

David has failed spectacularly. He knows he has failed God. But he also knows that the best place to go when you've failed God is to God himself. It would have been easy for David (as it is for us) to think, *I've really blown it. I can't possibly go anywhere near God now.* There's a sense in which that should be true: we're really not people who should have any business with a God who claims to be good.

But David has already learnt something about God, and it's right there in those opening lines. David is not crying out to God in utter desperation, thinking that even an outside chance that God would listen to him is better than nothing. No, David calls out to God based on what he knows God is like. David asks for mercy: for God to blot out and wash away all his wrongdoing. He asks God to treat him as if he had never done the things which he has done. But he asks God to do this not as a favour to a king but according to God's own ways—according to God's own "unfailing love" and "great compassion". These are words God has used to describe himself at key moments throughout the Old Testament. God advertises himself to be "the compassionate and gracious God, slow to anger, abounding in love and faithfulness" (Exodus 34 v 6). This is God's favourite way to speak of himself; it's his pinned tweet. It is at the very heart of who God is to be compassionate, gracious, loving and faithful.

David has learned this along the way. So he comes to God and asks for what is seemingly impossible because God has shown himself to be the kind of God who does impossibly kind things for people who don't deserve them at all.

We tend to think that if God loves us, it has to be because

we have made ourselves worthy of his love. But this is not the case. God loves us because of what *he's* like more than because of what *we're* like.[32] He loves us because he is utterly loving, not because we're utterly loveable.

David knew this, and we can know it too. None of us *deserve* God's love. But all of us can receive it. If David could, then we can. We're not so good that we don't need to come to God asking for mercy. And we're not so bad that we can't. Whatever we've done, whatever we've viewed, whatever we've thought. No amount of sexual sin is enough to mean you can't turn to God.

That God is like this is what makes Christianity good news. A God like this is one we can be honest with about our failings.

WHAT WE NEED TO ACKNOWLEDGE

We seem to live in an era of "non-apology" apologies. We're used to public figures "apologising" for how their words or actions made someone feel, or were interpreted, without them actually acknowledging any wrongdoing.

David doesn't do that. We've already seen that he admits what he has done is sinful. Not just unideal or imperfect but actually and morally wrong. A real ethical line exists. and David knows he has crossed it. As he says:

> *For I know my transgressions,*
> *and my sin is always before me.* PSALM 51 v 3

David not only knows that what he's done is wrong, but he also can't seem to get it out of his mind. Now that he has been confronted and the true nature of his actions exposed, his conscience is deeply troubled. He can't stop thinking

---

32 I owe this phrase, I think, to Glen Scrivener.

about what he's done. There's no sugar-coating. He doesn't call it a "misstep" or a "stumble". What he has done is "evil" in God's sight (v 4). There is no way around this.

Nor does David attempt to say that his deeds are entirely unrepresentative of what he's like. It's common these days when someone's wrong is exposed for them to say, "I don't know what came over me; this isn't who I am". David says the opposite:

> Surely I was sinful at birth,
> sinful from the time my mother conceived me.
>
> PSALM 51 v 5

Scholars debate whether David was using poetic exaggeration (hyperbole) here or whether he really believed he had a sinful nature even from the moment he was conceived. But David's basic point is clear: what he did was an outworking of what is deep within him. He committed adultery because he is, in his heart, an adulterer. He lied because he is, in his heart, a liar. He murdered because he is, in his heart, a murderer. David understands that this is a heart issue, not some one-off behavioural aberration. He did what he did because his heart is as it is.

This is a deeply uncomfortable realisation to come to terms with, but it is what we see throughout the teaching of Jesus. We instinctively want to make the issue our behaviour (which we trust can be improved); Jesus constantly challenges us to see that the issue is our heart.

As in most generations, we tend to think that who we are deep down is fundamentally good. We know (in our better, more realistic moments) that we don't get everything right. But it is something else entirely to admit there is something fundamentally wrong with us at our deepest core. Yet this is what Jesus insists we confront. On one occasion he issued this uncomfortable diagnosis:

> *For out of the heart come evil thoughts—murder,*
> *adultery, sexual immorality, theft, false testimony,*
> *slander. These are what defile a person.*
>
> MATTHEW 15 v 19-20

All the things Jesus lists are but symptoms of what is wrong underneath. We have evil thoughts because of what our hearts are like. We steal and lie because of what our hearts are like. And we misuse human sexuality (ours and other people's) because of what our hearts are like. Unless we acknowledge that, we will never truly understand ourselves. Our sexual brokenness is a sign of a deeper, more fundamental brokenness in our human nature.

Again, something of what God has proved himself to be makes it safe for David to admit that to him. David had seen from his own dealings with God, and from his people's long history of God, that his Lord really *is* gracious, compassionate and full of faithfulness and love.

We can know the same thing. These qualities of God—so clear to David in Old Testament times—are most clearly seen in the life of Jesus. As you read through any of the four Gospels, it is impossible to miss the kind of God Jesus reveals to us. A God who doesn't pretend we're better than we are, or simply scold us for being as we are, but amazingly steps into our reality and takes all our brokenness onto himself.

It was said of Jesus that "a bruised reed he will not break, and a smouldering wick he will not snuff out" (Matthew 12 v 20). Unfamiliar language, perhaps, but it expresses something truly wonderful. Jesus is tender enough for us to trust him with our most painful bruises. He won't crush us. He is more gentle with all our brokenness and failings than we can actually imagine.

This is the heart of the Christian faith. Because of what Jesus has done, it is now at last safe to be fully known by God. We don't need to hide. There's no need for spin. We can confess the worst things in our hearts deeply and freely.

WHAT WE NEED TO RECEIVE

David doesn't only acknowledge the reality of his heart (though this would not have been easy). He also comes before God and asks for help. He knows God does not just expose what we're truly like. That on its own would be no ultimate help. No, God also promises to work in our lives to make us new, so this is what David prays for:

> *Cleanse me ... wash me ...*
> *Let me hear joy and gladness ...*
> *Hide your face from my sins and blot out all my iniquity.*
> *Create in me a pure heart, O God.*   PSALM 51 v 7-10

David asked that God, somehow, would not count his sins against him. He knew God could do this—find some way to take the wrong we have done and yet not treat us as such wrongs deserve. Now, the death of Jesus shows us how.

David also asked for a new, cleaner heart. Forgiveness is one thing, but change is another.

Some years ago a friend and I were hiking on a mountain in Snowdonia in Wales. The route was getting busy, so we decided to "improvise" our own way to the top, which would avoid all the other hikers. At one point we dropped down onto a ledge, and there didn't seem any way down or back up. I began to get anxious, and I remember saying to myself, "If I ever get out of this, I'm never going to do something so stupid ever again". Which was ironic, because it wasn't the first time I had said something like that. A few years earlier something remarkably similar had happened on a mountain in England's Lake District.

So at that moment in Wales, I needed to be rescued from two things: the ledge, and my stupid propensity to get myself into these situations. I needed rescue *and* change. Without the latter I would presumably end up on another ledge on some other mountain range in the not-too-distant future.

It's not enough to say to God, "I wish I hadn't done that". What we really need to say is, "I wish I wasn't the kind of person who does that".

The good news is that God doesn't forgive us without also transforming us. And in fact it is the very forgiveness he extends that ends up changing us. As we learn that Christ took our sin on himself, we start to have a different attitude to it. It is not that we are incapable of sin, but that it doesn't taste as good. It is like drinking orange juice after you've just brushed your teeth. The juice hasn't changed, but your palate dramatically has. The death of Christ has that effect on us. If we turn to Jesus, we will find that sin gradually loses its flavour.

This is so important to know. It is easy to believe we will never change. It may be we have really developed certain sexual habits we don't believe it will ever be possible to break. Maybe it is accessing porn, or hooking up with strangers, or moving from one sexual relationship to another, or routinely fantasizing about particular individuals. It seems so ingrained. We can't imagine not wanting to do this, let alone actually changing our behaviour.

So, like David, we actually need to ask for joy—"Let me hear joy and gladness" (v 8). Sin attacks our joy. It makes life miserable. But spiritual joy also attacks our sin. We only finally stop enjoying a sin when we start to enjoy something else far more. It is hard to switch off an unhealthy desire; we need a new and greater desire. So David doesn't want to grit his teeth and follow God's ways. He wants to love and want those ways.

We can ask God for all these things. Jesus makes it clear that God loves to give good gifts to his children (see Matthew 7 v 7-11). If we find ourselves wanting nothing of God's ways, we can tell him. We can *want* to want them.

None of us is good enough not to need this. And none of us is bad enough not to be able to find it. That God can forgive and renew a man like David shows he can do the same for anyone. It is painful coming to terms with what the Bible says about our sexuality being so broken. But such recognition is the way into the joy of knowing forgiveness and transformation.

FRESH EVERY DAY

One of my favourite childhood memories is of visiting my grandparents by the sea. Their house was right by a vast sandy beach, and the retreating tide would leave what seemed (to my young eyes) to be miles of streams and lakes. I'd spend many hours shovelling in the sand: damming up the bigger rivers, creating new reservoirs, building walls and defences. By the end of an afternoon, the beach would look dramatically re-engineered. I'd be exhausted, a little bronzed in the sun and very happy with my work.

But one thing was guaranteed. The next morning, there would be no evidence at all of the hours of labour the day before. The tide would have come and gone, and the beach completely reset. I'd have a new canvas on which to work.

It can be hard to imagine that the wreckage of this broken world can ever be tidied up. Some of us are conscious of the deep mess we have made of other people. We think of hurts we have caused, ways in which we have used our sexuality and theirs selfishly. We think of the mess all this has made in our own hearts, let alone other people's.

David may have felt the same way. But he knew the compassion and kindness of God. He knew that God's response to our mess is not simply to trash us—though he would be well within his rights to—but to help us. David knew that, like the tide on the beach, God is quite able and willing to wash away all our wrongdoing. So, when he acknowledges what he has done, asks for help, and knows that the God he is praying to is trigger-happy with compassion, David can be confident of the outcome. And so can we.

We are all sexual sinners. You are. And so am I. I can think of things I have thought about, and things that I have done that even now bring me great shame. It can take very little for my mind to start thinking of others in a way that does not honour their sexuality: a way that dehumanises and commodifies them. There is real perversion in my heart. It grieves me. But at times it still tempts me. I'm not done fighting this, and I'm not done growing. I guess I will be conscious of this and battling for the rest of my life. I will always have a faulty sexuality.

So I need this good news of Christianity. I need to know that God's capacity to forgive and heal is far greater than my capacity to mess things up. I need to know that he is big enough, clever enough and *good* enough to look at the mess of my heart and actions, and draw near to me in Christ, to invite me to himself, and to start the process of putting me back together. That's a message I need to hear every day.

It's good news that God cares about this area of life. The alternative is to leave us to our own devices, which doesn't bear thinking about. But that doesn't mean it is easy to trust him with this. For many of us, sex and sexuality feel like the key means of self-expression and self-realisation. So let's look at what Jesus does for someone whose core mission and identity has become finding the right partner, and who was convinced this would be the key to the fullest life. Her encounter doesn't put her off Jesus—quite the opposite. He is good news for those who are sexually damaged—and for those who have done the damaging.

Don't we need to be sexually fulfilled to be who we are?

Think about everything you've had to drink so far today. It may have started with coffee and juice at breakfast, and then maybe a few glasses of water through the day, or a couple more coffees or cups of tea. We tend not to think about it precisely because we don't typically need to. We barely give it a moment's consideration: whatever we usually want and need to drink is so readily available. We grab it without a second thought. Which means that we don't really know what it means to be thirsty. Not really.

Thirst is such a primary need and basic concept that we often use it to speak of other needs and desires. We talk about someone having a thirst for companionship or knowledge, or a child being able to soak up information like a sponge, or wanting to drink in the view at a scenic spot.

It is not surprising, then, that we easily use this sort of language when speaking about sex as well. We think of it as a matter of desires, appetites, needs, and of wanting to find satisfaction. Intense cravings can obviously cause problems. Extreme thirst might cause a shipwrecked sailor to drink salty seawater when it will only deepen the experience of thirst. We see this too when it comes to sexual cravings. Regrettable sexual encounters are often the result of deep unmet desires that we then look to fulfil in ways that ultimately don't help.

THE WOMAN AT THE WELL

All of this helps us as we encounter a woman from a very different time and place to our own. She was in a region known as Samaria in present-day Israel. And we can assume she knew a lot about real physical thirst, because we meet her in the middle of the day, when the sun is at its height and the air at its hottest. She was there two thousand years ago. When we meet her, she is physically thirsty, approaching a well for some water, and physically alone—isolated and ostracised. So we can assume she knows about the thirst for companionship too. When we leave her, both of these thirsts have been met.

Her time and place might not be familiar to us, but much of her experience will be. She has a complicated sexual history—in fact one that would have been scandalous in her day, and the reason she is shunned. She lives with unmet desires. Her love life has been a string of failed attempts to meet those desires. She's a mess. Maybe by this point she is wondering if there is any hope of fulfilment.

We only know about her because she ran into Jesus Christ, and the whole episode is recorded for us in one of the four Gospels—you can read the account in John 4 v 1-30.

There is a sense in which Jesus shouldn't have been there. Jews tended not to travel through Samaria. There was bad history between the two peoples, and many Jews wouldn't even want their feet to touch Samaritan soil. They would travel the long way around to avoid having to pass through it. But Jesus had his own way of thinking about these things. As he journeys through the region, he stops at a well in a town called, Sychar, and, John tells us, it is noon—the middle of the day. This is where he meets this particular woman.

She shouldn't really have been there either. The middle of the day was the worst time to be outside. People would normally make a trip to the well in the early hours when it was cooler. That she is here at such an antisocial hour suggests she doesn't mix in the usual circles. That she's heading there on her own suggests she might not mix in any circles.

Jesus opens by asking her for some water:

> *Will you give me a drink?*   JOHN 4 v 7

This shouldn't have happened either. In that culture, men didn't generally talk to women they didn't know. But in this case it was even worse: he was a Jewish rabbi, and she was a Samaritan woman of apparent disrepute. Jesus is smashing through all sorts of social, ethnic, moral, religious and gender barriers. This encounter will tell us a lot about him. She may well be an outcast on her own in an otherwise deserted place, but Jesus in no way takes advantage of her or has a go at her. He treats her with respect and dignity.

THE MAN AT THE WELL

It is worth pausing on this for a moment. While Jesus was in many ways a part of first-century Jewish culture, he wasn't bound by it. He didn't simply go along with the flow just because it was the culture of the time. He was prepared to radically break with custom when he felt it necessary. His commitment to Old Testament sexual ethics is therefore not a sign that he was helplessly trapped in the culture of his day.

SAM ALLBERRY

This is, by the way, exactly what we would expect from someone who claims to be who Jesus claims to be—the One sent from his Father in heaven to draw people to him. If he truly has been sent from heaven, then he comes from outside all human culture and so his words and teaching will at times affirm, and at other times critique, the values of any particular human culture. It is a sign that he doesn't fully belong to any one cultural moment, including the one he was born into and raised in. He is in it but not of it (something he calls his followers to be).

So, unlike many of his contemporaries, he does not think this woman is beneath him. Quite the opposite. He doesn't withdraw from the disreputable. He seeks them out.

There follows a short exchange:

> *The Samaritan woman said to him, "You are a Jew and I am a Samaritan woman. How can you ask me for a drink?"*
>
> *... Jesus answered her, "If you knew the gift of God and who it is that asks you for a drink, you would have asked him and he would have given you living water."*   JOHN 4 v 9-10

This is typical of the sort of thing Jesus says, and it highlights why he so often confounds our expectations. Each part of what he says to her is significant:

- *"If you knew the gift of God..."* Jesus is saying that there is something God has which is available to anyone as a gift: something which is not deserved or earned or merited. Receiving it is not contingent on our race, or our gender, or our character and performance.
- *"... and who it is that asks you for a drink, you would have*

asked him..." Whatever it is that God has for us is available from Christ himself, and it's there for the asking. He has the authority to give us what God wants for us.

- *"... and he would have given you living water."* The gift that's available to us from God, through Jesus, is "living water". Jesus was standing at a well in an arid country. Water was never far from people's consciousness. Thirst was not an occasional and mild discomfort; it was a perpetual and serious threat. The location, availability and supply of water governed much of everyday life. Water is life. We don't naturally appreciate how extraordinarily dependent we are on it, and what it would be to try to live without easy access to it. And yet, for all the centrality of water to life, Jesus is saying that there is something in addition we can have—"living water."

Jesus goes on to explain what he means by this:

> *Jesus answered, "Everyone who drinks this water will be thirsty again, but whoever drinks the water I give them will never thirst. Indeed, the water I give them will become in them a spring of water welling up to eternal life."*   JOHN 4 v 13-14

Jesus is making a huge claim: that there are two kinds of water. The normal kind—the kind this woman was drawing from this well—and the water Jesus himself offers.

Normal water is great for what it does, but what it does is somewhat limited. It quenches our thirst but only temporarily. This woman will take what she needs and gladly use it, but she will need to come back for more. She will never be able to take enough. It is the same for us. However much water we can get hold of, we will always need more.

But Jesus says our daily water is not the only kind of water there is. And our thirst for it is not the only kind of thirst we feel. There is another, deeper thirst.

WHAT WE ARE THIRSTY FOR

The "living water" Jesus offers *can* provide ultimate satisfaction. Once we have this water, there will be no more of this thirst. Its effect will be lasting and permanent.

Jesus says his water is internal. He describes a spring that will be found *within* us if we drink this water: a spring "*in* them." No need to find a nearby well. It will somehow be in our own hearts. And not just an inner well, notice, but an inner *spring*. The two are not the same. A well can be closed off and opened up. It provides water when it is needed. But a spring is a perpetual source. It cannot be switched on and off. We don't control it. So whatever this living water is, Jesus is not just promising a quantity large enough to live on for the rest of our lives but an actual never-ending, internal supply. We become not just recipients but carriers.

Jesus is saying there is a thirst that afflicts us all. A deep inner thirst. A thirst of the soul. A thirst he says *he alone* can quench and satisfy. All of us experience this—an ache, a yearning for something that seems always beyond our reach. C.S. Lewis describes it as a desire each of us has for a "far-off country". It is deeply personal. Lewis continues:

> *In speaking of this desire for our own far-off country, which we find in ourselves even now, I feel a certain shyness. I am almost committing an indecency. I am trying to rip open the inconsolable secret in each one of you ... the secret ... which pierces with such sweetness that when, in very intimate conversation, the mention of it becomes imminent, we grow awkward and affect to laugh at ourselves; the secret we cannot hide and cannot*

tell, though we desire to do both. We cannot tell it be-cause it is a desire for something that has never actually appeared in our experience. We cannot hide it because our experience is constantly suggesting it, and we betray ourselves like lovers at the mention of a name. [33]

All of us have our own conception of what this is, and our own quiet way of seeking it. But Jesus' claim is that nothing we can find or achieve for ourselves will ever satisfy it. Whatever we seek to fill that void won't be enough. The more we have of it, the more we will continue to want of it, whether that's relationships, power, intimacy, family, money, recognition, security, or anything else.

The magnate and philanthropist John D. Rockefeller, when asked how much money would be enough, famously replied, "Just a little bit more". We tend to roll our eyes at the absurdity of this, given how fantastically wealthy he was, but Jesus is implying that the same is exactly true of us. Wherever we look to satisfy our soul-thirst, there will never be enough of it to provide true relief. There's not enough money in the world for someone who lives for riches. There's not enough intimacy for someone who lives for connection, or recognition for someone who lives for their reputation. There is not enough of anything, anywhere in the world, to quench the thirst that Jesus says lies in the heart of us all.

This explains why success in life can so often, and so sur-prisingly, lead to boredom and deep restlessness. If we final-ly arrive at the destination we have dreamed of for our life, it feels wonderful for a few moments, but then the sense comes that there's somewhere a bit further we need to get to in order to be *really* happy.

---

33   C.S. Lewis, *The Weight of Glory* (William Collins, 2013), p 29-30.

SAM ALLBERRY

There is evidence of this all around us. If we doubt this, it is probably because we haven't yet arrived at the place we imagine will make us satisfied. But those who do tell the same story. It isn't enough. They need something more. There are people who have earned an absurd amount of money, or bedded an absurd number of people, or attained an absurd number of degrees and qualifications, and who still feel as though they need more than this. It is never ending.

Jesus shows us why. The presence of a thirst for something we can't find in this world shows we are made for something outside of this world. Again, C.S. Lewis hits the nail on the head:

> *If we find ourselves with a desire that nothing in this world can satisfy, the most probable explanation is that we were made for another world.*[34]

This is exactly what Jesus is saying: he has come to provide something from outside this world that our hearts and souls crave.

This is what Jesus claims to possess and now offers to this lone Samaritan woman at the well. Abruptly in the middle of their conversation—rudely, perhaps, to our ears—he asks her to bring her husband to him. She answers that she has no husband. It feels awkward to us—a little like asking when someone's baby is due only to find out she isn't pregnant. But Jesus knows what he is doing. He is carefully bringing into the open what her heart has been trusting in all these years:

34   C.S. Lewis *Mere Christianity* (Macmillan, 1956) p 20.

> *Jesus said to her, "You are right when you say you have*
> *no husband. The fact is, you have had five husbands,*
> *and the man you now have is not your husband. What*
> *you have just said is quite true."*   JOHN 4 v 17-18

Jesus knew this all along—it seems to have been a super-natural insight. He's raised this painful matter with her not because he's being cruel but because, having shown her the availability of this living water, he wants to reveal her specific need for it.

She has been married five times. She is now with a new man: one who at this stage is not her husband. Why bring this up? Because this is where her need for living water is most apparent. These men are how she has been trying to quench her soul-thirst. Each time she has thought that maybe *this* man will be the one to bring satisfaction. It hasn't worked out for the first five, but maybe number six will be the one?

It is a tragic story. These attempts at finding her deepest satisfaction in relationships are demonstrably failing to work.

But we need to bear something else in mind. In the ancient world, it was men and not women who could initiate divorce. Each of those failed marriages has ended at the instigation of the man, and not her. So we mustn't think of her as someone who repeatedly cast men aside when they weren't enough for her. *They* were the ones to end it. Five times in her life a man has decided that she is not someone they want to be married to any longer. Think about that. *Five times.* That is an incalculable amount of rejection to go through.

These two things—her looking for ultimate satisfaction through relationship and her being serially rejected—may not be unrelated. The fact is, if we marry someone, or even just get together with them, thinking that this will be what will fulfil us, we won't be very easy to live with. If we expect another human being to be able to fill that amount of purpose and meaning in our lives, it will easily place an unbearable burden on them. The more pressure we put on our relationship, the more fearful we will become of losing it, more jealous of anyone else who might impinge on it, more resentful of the ways it doesn't seem to be delivering, and more paranoid about potential threats to it. So perhaps it's not just that these men weren't enough for the Samaritan woman; *she* was also too much for them.

So she has two needs. She doesn't just need to find someone who can meet her expectations and satisfy these unrealistic needs. She also needs to find someone who won't use her or reject her. This means that she needs to find someone who can actually bear the full weight of her needs without being crushed by this burden of them. According to Jesus, that person is standing right in front of her. If she knew who Jesus really was, she would be asking *him* for living water.

As the conversation goes on, Jesus reiterates his point:

> *Yet a time is coming and has now come when the true worshippers will worship the Father in the Spirit and in truth, for they are the kind of worshippers the Father seeks.*　　　JOHN 4 v 23

God is seeking a heart relationship with people.

This is obviously deep stuff, and not easy for us to get our heads around. This is certainly the case for the Samaritan Jesus is speaking to.

> *The woman said, "I know that Messiah" (called Christ) "is coming. When he comes, he will explain everything to us."*　　　JOHN 4 v 25

Jesus has one more thing to say to her, and it will end up changing her life entirely.

> *Then Jesus declared, "I, the one speaking to you—I am he."*
> JOHN 4 v 26

There it is. One short sentence. But even sentences can change lives, and this one turned hers upside down.

Jesus is saying he is the one she is waiting for so expectantly. He is the one who will tell the people all things. In fact, this is precisely what he has been doing. He has been telling her that God has a gift for her: a gift that will be the answer to a whole life of fruitless and heart breaking searching. He's been showing her that she needs living water, for peace and satisfaction in her soul. He has been explaining how God is in fact seeking worshippers—even her. All of this Jesus has been opening up to her.

But there is something else this final comment crystallises. Try as she might to avoid the issue, Jesus has been opening her up to herself too. He has made sense of her. He has accounted for the trajectory of her life and the parched feeling deep inside of her. He has shown her why she has such an unyielding ache inside her, and where she can finally find the answer to her longing. She's been looking for ultimate satisfaction in a man. What she really needs is what only Jesus can offer her: *living water.*

THIRST QUENCHING

We need to know this. For many in our culture, sex or romantic connection is the way we try to quench the thirst of our souls. That's why it matters so much to us. It's what we feel we need. It is why we are so cautious about a belief system, like Christianity, that might restrict who we sleep with. But to seek our ultimate satisfaction in sexual or romantic fulfilment is to keep drinking the salt water of this world. It will never truly quench our thirst. No relationship or sexual experience will ever be enough.

So how does this living water of Jesus actually work? What is he really speaking about?

Jesus is ultimately talking about his death. When the Samaritan woman leaves him after this encounter, she is dramatically changed. When we first met her, she was a thirsty outcast, on her way to the well to find water at a time when she would be guaranteed to avoid people. But as she heads off after meeting Jesus, it is very different. She heads back to her town to tell the people there about Jesus. They had shunned her, and she had avoided them. Now she seeks them and they find her compelling, following her to meet Jesus (v 30). It is a complete reversal.

And in a telling detail we see another change. As she got up to leave, John notes that she left her water jar at the well and didn't take it with her (v 28). The one thing she came for she had now forgotten about. She was no longer thirsty.

How was Jesus able to bring about this change in her?

What he went through in his death tells us. In his death he became the ultimate outcast, cruelly targeted by his enemies, misunderstood by his family, crushed by the authorities, abandoned by his friends and alienated from God, crying out, "My God, my God, why have you forsaken me?" (Mark 15:34).

In his death he also experienced spiritual thirst. For the very first time he lacked something in God that he had never lacked before. He experienced the ultimate thirst of the soul, becoming parched of the living water he had earlier been offering to this woman. He cried out, "I am thirsty" from the cross (John 19 v 28) as a sign of not just his physical torment but of the deeper spiritual agony he was going through.

Why? Because he was taking our place. He was excluded from God in the way that we deserve to be, so that we can be welcomed into relationship with him. He experienced the spiritual thirst that our spiritual barrenness leads to so that we can be drenched in the living water of soul-satisfying fellowship with God that we all most deeply need and truly crave.

WHAT DOES JESUS OFFER?

This is what it is to receive Jesus' living water, and it leads to three things.

The first is realising we are known and loved by God.

All of us long to be known and loved. It's why romantic and sexual experience matters so much to us. But often in life we are forced to choose between the two: either being fully loved or being fully known. The two often feel in tension to us.

The risk we all face in this world is that the more we are known, the less we might be loved as a consequence. We worry that if people really knew us, they wouldn't love us. And we worry that those who most love us only do so because they don't fully know us. And so we spend much of our lives filtering what others see of us and know of us. We edit the image people encounter and the behaviour they witness. It can be exhausting living like this.

This is what had happened to the Samaritan woman. The men who knew her most intimately had rejected her. Her own community had ostracised her. But Jesus didn't. When he saw her at the well, he did not withdraw in disgust or stick around only to scold her. He initiated a relationship with her. And not because he didn't know her well enough to be put off by her. He already knew her story, warts and all. And yet, despite knowing her so deeply, he still came to her in love.

The musical *Dear Evan Hansen* opened on Broadway in 2016 and went on to win a slew of awards and to be adapted into a bestselling novel. Its title character struggles to connect with others, and so (at the suggestion of his therapist) he writes a letter to himself about how things are going to be ok. Another college student finds the letter and proceeds to mock him for it. But when this student takes his own life, his parents find the letter still on him, and assume he wrote it to Hansen and that the two of them must have had a deep connection. Evan Hansen suddenly finds himself being noticed and celebrated, having apparently befriended a struggling student and been his sole support. For the first time he finds himself connecting with others, especially the dead student's family. But it is all based on a lie—one that eventually unravels.

At a key moment of despair for Hansen, his mother says to him, "I love you." He responds, "You don't even know me. No one does." She then replies, "I know you, and I love you." When I saw the show a few months ago, there was not a dry eye in the house. It was incredibly powerful. We all long to be deeply known and deeply loved, at the same time.

The strapline for the show is "You will be found". It sums up the story of the Samaritan.

Jesus knew her. He knew her better than she even knew herself. And he loved her. He reached out to her. He offered her the living water of his own life. Jesus knows us the most fully and yet loves us the most deeply.

WHAT JESUS WANTS

Secondly, Jesus does this not out of some sense of duty but out of a deep desire for us to know him.

His disciples eventually rejoin him, having gone away to find food for lunch. When they return they're confused as Jesus doesn't seem to be hungry. Jesus explains:

> *"I have food to eat that you know nothing about."*
>
> JOHN 4 v 32

They're still confused, so he explains:

> *"My food," said Jesus, "is to do the will of him who sent me and to finish his work."* JOHN 4 v 34

Jesus is saying this at the very point when a whole load of Samaritans are on their way to find him, persuaded by the Samaritan woman. *This* is that work. Many of them are about to believe in him (v 39), to find in him the same living water and soul-satisfaction he has offered the woman. This is why Jesus has been sent into the world. This is what the Father has for him to do.

And Jesus says that doing this—pouring himself out for the sake of others—is *food* to him. It is entirely why he is no longer thinking about his need for lunch. The real water he has to offer isn't found in a well, and the real food for him isn't found in the local supermarket.

This is how Jesus feels about drawing near to us and bringing us to the Father. Our satisfaction is to be found in coming to him, rather than in any kind of sexual or romantic fantasy finally being realised. And his satisfaction is found in drawing us to God.

SEEING OURSELVES

Thirdly, his love entirely reshapes how we see ourselves.

After meeting him, the woman said, "Come, see a man who told me everything I've ever done. Could this be the Messiah?" (v 28). Her encounter with Jesus made sense of her in a way that she never could have made sense of herself. She now saw herself in a different light.

She was not the only one. John, the author of the Gospel and this account, also found his view of himself utterly reshaped by knowing Jesus. In a few places where he turns up in the narrative, he refers to himself as "the disciple Jesus loved". He doesn't mean this in an obnoxious way, as if to suggest that he was loved by Jesus more than the other disciples were. I take it he means it in a sense of wonder—that he's never quite got over the fact that Jesus loves *him*.

We tend to find our identity in who we most love. It is why sexuality has such a powerful effect on our identity. The sort of attractions we experience, and the sort of people we feel attracted to, easily form a key (or *the* key) to who we understand ourselves to be. Sexual identity has become a powerful force in Western society. We typically assume that people have a fundamental right to whatever sexual identity they think best describes who they are. We have made sexuality the foundation to self-understanding. Sexual behaviour has therefore become a primary means of self-expression. To restrict sexual behaviour is to stop someone from being who they are.

But this is a very problematic way to think. If we are defined by our sexual and romantic desires, then we are really saying that our sexual desires need to be met in order for us to fully be ourselves; your ability to be authentically and fully you is contingent on being able to lead a sexually and romantically fulfilled life.

The problem with this is that it leads us to think that a life without this is barely a life worth living: that those who, for any reason, are unable to fulfil their sexual desires are missing out on the one true chance they have of being fully who they are. We need to realise how damaging this message could be to someone. It raises the stakes dangerously high. To say to someone that the person they sleep with is their primary means of self-expression is to imply that a sexually unfulfilled life is no real life at all. This sort of pressure is only going to add to the emotional pressure felt by those who are encouraged to make sexuality their core identity.

John shows us a better way to think about this. He does not find his ultimate identity in the person he most loves. He finds his ultimate identity in the person who has most loved him—in Jesus.[35] God cares who we sleep with because that's where we've massively and unhelpfully invested our identity.

This, above all else, is the love that can truly define us and explain us. This is the love that most matters. All of which goes to show that we might not have understood love quite as much as we think we have, as we shall see.

---

35 I am thankful to Jojo Ruba for this insight.

Isn't love enough?

The political drama *The West Wing* followed the lives of staffers in the White House. The main characters are the advisors, aides and communications team, which surround the president on a daily basis. In one particular episode, the president is in the early stages of running for re-election for a second term in office. A frontrunner is emerging from the opposing party, and one day he's asked what makes him want to be president. To the delight of the White House staff, he gives an incoherent, feeble answer:

> *The reason I would run, were I to run, is I have a great belief in this country as a country and in this people as a people that go into making this country a nation with the greatest natural resources and population of people, educated people.* [36]

But the delight of the staff quickly evaporates when one of them asks if *they* have a good answer to the same question, and they begin to realise they don't—and that it's surprisingly

---

36 "Gone Quiet", *The West Wing*, Season 3, Episode 7.

difficult to come up with one. "Why do you want to be president?" feels as if it should be easy to answer, until they try to answer it.

You've probably not had to try to answer *that* question, so here's another that is much closer to home: "What is love?"

Once again, it feels so obvious that we don't need to think about it. It is only when we do stop and think about it that we realise it isn't obvious at all.

WHAT WE KNOW AND DON'T KNOW

We know so much about love that we don't realise how much we don't know about it.

We know it matters. We know we can't live without it. This is so intuitive we don't stop to think about why it is so obviously the case. It just is. Whatever our worldview or politics or belief system or cultural background, we all know that life is, in some sense, about love. It is what makes life work. We sense that without love, everything else loses much of its point and purpose. We read about some celebrity who is fabulously wealthy but utterly alone, and we realise that the wealth is not worth it if this is what it costs. Or we see people who are spectacularly successful but only through trampling over many others along the way, and we sense that some things matter more than being successful.

But while this is incontestable, something else is also apparent. We don't find it easy to pin down exactly what love *is*. We know it is there. We know it matters enormously. We know we need it and aren't meant to live without it. But what it actually *is* is surprisingly difficult to articulate.

This actually matters. Most of what we think about sex is based on the assumption that it is all about love. When there are discussions in our culture over issues like the definition of marriage or Christian beliefs about who we sleep with, arguments tend to revolve around lines like "You can't regulate love", or hashtags like *#Loveislove* and *#Equallove*. Love is the bottom line in all this. If you look like you're against love, you've already lost the argument. And because (on this understanding) sex is love, anything that seems to curtail sexual freedom is accused of being unloving.

But we're assuming we know what we're talking about. And if it transpires we're actually *unclear* on exactly what love is, then these arguments don't mean as much as we thought. In fact, we find our thinking has very little foundation if our view of love turns out to be purely subjective. If it matters who we sleep with, we really need a solid basis for how we think about it.

We're actually in a predicament. We know enough to know that love matters, but not enough to know what it *is*. It seems vital, for sure. But it's also elusive. It's a little like trying to follow an old road atlas where a coffee stain has obliterated the destination. You know you need to get there; you're just not exactly sure where it is.

So let's look at some of the fundamental things the Bible says about love.

1. Love really does matter

One of the most famous parts of the Bible is a poem about love. Many people who've never touched a Bible in their lives are familiar with it. It has become iconic. Barack Obama referenced part of it in his first inaugural address. Countless weddings have used it as a reading. British Prime Minister Tony Blair read it at Princess Diana's funeral in 1997. The Rolling Stones adapted it, and Macklemore's hit song (and LGBT rights anthem) *Same Love* quotes part of it.

Here's how it starts:

*If I speak in the tongues of men or of angels, but
do not have love, I am only a resounding gong or a
clanging cymbal. If I have the gift of prophecy and can
fathom all mysteries and all knowledge, and if I have a
faith that can move mountains, but do not have love,
I am nothing. If I give all I possess to the poor and give
over my body to hardship that I may boast, but do not
have love, I gain nothing.*

1 Corinthians 13 v 1-3

The apostle Paul shows that, however impressive you may
be, none of it matters if you are unloving. The Christians
to whom Paul is writing are fascinated with the possibility
of speaking in spiritual languages or tongues. So Paul ups
the ante. Suppose you could speak in the tongues of *angels*?
How awesome would *that* be?

But without love, it is nothing. It is like a clanging cymbal.
It is just noise, like a car alarm blaring out in the middle of
the night. Without love, even an ability like this is entirely
useless.

The same is true of how much we know. Imagine you
could understand "all mysteries and all knowledge". Suppose you could answer all the big questions about life? But
once again, even all knowledge in the mind of someone who
is unloving is not worth it. Paul says it is *you* that is nothing.
Where there should be a personality, there is just a blank
space. You can have so much and be a complete nothing at
the same time. It is as if the very process of living an unloving life erases your self. What a thought.

And love matters more than sacrifice. Paul thinks of some
of the most dramatic things you might do for some precious

cause. You might give away everything that you have, even your life. But Paul says it is possible to do all this—without love.

So whatever we're talking about—abilities, talents, skills, successes, achievements, sacrifices—any and even all of it without love comes to naught. Anything minus love = nothing. That's how essential love is.

A life with no love is no life at all.

So far so good. But now it starts to get a little more difficult.

2. We're not as loving as we think

In the next part of this passage on love, Paul starts to describe love:

> *Love is patient, love is kind. It does not envy, it does*
> *not boast, it is not proud. It does not dishonour others,*
> *it is not self-seeking, it is not easily angered, it keeps*
> *no record of wrongs. Love does not delight in evil*
> *but rejoices with the truth. It always protects, always*
> *trusts, always hopes, always perseveres.*
>
> 1 Corinthians 13 v 4-7

Paul uses both positive and negative language—we see what love *is* and what it is *not*. Negative comparisons often provide sharp moments of clarity. Paul concludes: "love ... always protects, always trusts, always hopes, always perseveres". There is nothing fickle or fleeting about it. It is consistent and dependable. It sticks around.

We probably don't object to any of these short statements about love. Many of them may seem like common sense, or so obvious it doesn't really need to be said. But by putting them together, there is a cumulative effect. It shows us how superficial our thinking about love can become. Paul shows us love is more than just action. But it is also more than just sentiment.

When we look back on Paul's words as a whole, something uncomfortable and unavoidable begins to become clear. We're not really like this. We want love, we approve of love, we esteem and celebrate it. But we're just not that good at doing it.

I'll show you. Look again at these words describing love.

Love is patient, love is kind. It does not envy, it does not boast, it is not proud. It does not dishonour others, it is not self-seeking, it is not easily angered, it keeps no record of wrongs. Love does not delight in evil but rejoices with the truth. It always protects, always trusts, always hopes, always perseveres.

Now substitute your own name for the word *love* and see how it sounds. This is what it becomes with mine:

Sam is patient, Sam is kind. Sam does not envy, Sam does not boast, Sam is not proud. Sam does not dishonour others, Sam is not self-seeking, Sam is not easily angered, Sam keeps no record of wrongs. Sam does not delight in evil but rejoices with the truth. Sam always protects, always trusts, always hopes, always perseveres.[37]

Honestly, it doesn't sound good. I promise you, anyone who knows me at all well would laugh out loud at these words.

So how about you? Does it sound any better?

This is actually the point of the passage. Paul, evil genius that he is, is not trying to inspire us all to feel amazing about love. He is actually trying to show us our own lack of it.

There is a deep and painful irony here. We believe in love. But we're not as loving as we thought. We're actually (if we're honest) quite unloving.

---

37 I first came across this insight from the British preacher Dick Lucas.

C.S. Lewis wrote a science-fiction novel in which the main character, Ransom, encounters an angelic being from another planet. Ransom describes the effect this encounter has on him:

> *I felt sure that the creature was what we call "good," but I wasn't sure whether I liked "goodness" so much as I had supposed. This is a very terrible experience. As long as what you are afraid of is something evil, you may still hope that the good may come to your rescue. But suppose you struggle through to the good and find that it also is dreadful? How if food itself turns out to be the very thing you can't eat, and home the very place you can't live, and your very comforter the person who makes you uncomfortable? Then, indeed, there is no rescue possible: the last card has been played. For a second or two I was nearly in that condition. Here at last was a bit of that world from beyond the world, which I had always supposed that I loved and desired, breaking through and appearing to my senses: and I didn't like it, I wanted it to go away.*[38]

The same could be said about discovering what love really is. It is the very thing we had assumed we would want and like. Yet when we see love as it truly is, we realise we aren't as at home with it as we thought we would be.

Paul's point is not that we're entirely *un*loving. We see beautiful and genuine acts of love all around us. But we're not as good at this love thing as we like to think we are. It is not our natural tendency to love in the way we're meant to. We need some outside help.

---

38   C.S. Lewis, *Perelandra* (New York: Scribner, 2003), p 17.

3. We need God's help

It is a common and understandable argument from many atheists that we don't need God to be good. After all, we are daily surrounded by instances of love and kindness from those of a variety of backgrounds and certainly including unbelievers. Whenever a catastrophe hits, there are always examples of heroic and selfless love. No one thinks to assume it must mean that these people believe in God.

But while there is a basic morality in most of us (something the Bible itself accounts for), it is still true that we need help to know what it means to be loving. The Bible grounds this in a famous assertion of just three monosyllables: "God is love".

This is how John puts it:

> *Dear friends, let us love one another, for love comes from God. Everyone who loves has been born of God and knows God. Whoever does not love does not know God, because God is love.*   1 JOHN 4 v 7-8

It is easy to misunderstand this. It doesn't mean that everything I think is love God must approve of. As we'll see, it is very easy for us to mistake all sorts of intense and even harmful feelings for love. To assume that God automatically endorses our understandings of love is actually to invert the passage and say that love is God.

What John is saying is that God knows far more about love than we do, and that we therefore need to listen to him if we are to love each other as well as we can. It means we cannot hope to love people in the best way without learning what God says that should look like.

God knows more about love because, John says, God *is* love.

This is not just saying that God is really good at love, as though everyone has a go at being loving but God is better at it than all others. A few years ago someone introduced me to a Chinese version of checkers. As it happens, I was really good at it. It was a surprise to me as much as to my friend. But this is not what we're talking about with God and love. It's not that love is this thing that is external to God and he just happens to be really good at it.

No. What the Bible is claiming is that God actually *is* love. He didn't come up with it one day, because that would mean it was something he didn't exhibit until a certain point. Saying God is love is saying that it is fundamental to him. It is not just something he *does* (even if he does it really well) but something he *is*. He never has to switch it on or work himself up to it. It naturally flows from his heart.

So love is God's expertise. And it means we need his help to know how to love others.

The fact is, most of us recognise that there is more than one way to love, and that different contexts call for different types of love. Consider the following statements:

- I love my mother.
- I love my spouse.
- I love my dog.
- I love sausages.

Each statement uses the same word but we instinctively understand it in differing ways appropriate to its object. Each is a love, but the loves are different. In fact we would say they are *necessarily* different. Love for a spouse should look very different to love for a parent. And love for a parent should look very different to love for a pet. We know this. And people who don't, tend to end up being the subject of documentaries.

In other words, it really won't do to use the slogan *#Loveislove* as a justification for a particular relationship. There are different forms of love, and loving well in any given situation involves ordering those loves appropriately. We combine or confuse them at our peril.

There are times when this is obvious to us. We might sense that one form of love is straying into another, less appropriate form. What is meant only to be a friendship starts to cross over into something sort of romantic. Or we sense that we are becoming too dependent on a parent in a way that's unhealthy. Or we see someone trying to have "human" companionship with a pet. It's why we need God's help. He will show us what love should look like in each and every context and situation.

And what he shows us will always be more loving than any alternative we might come up with. Obedience to him will never mean we end up loving people less. We might feel like that in some cases, but that is probably because we are wanting to love someone in the wrong kind of way, and God isn't so much calling us to love them *less* as to love them *differently*, which will really mean loving them *more*.

TAINTED LOVE

There is a chilling illustration of this in the Bible. In 2 Samuel 13 we read a horrific account of the rape by Amnon of his half-sister Tamar. At the start of the account, Amnon confides to a friend, "I love Tamar, my brother Absalom's sister" (v 4). The language is very telling. He says he loves her, but the unfolding events utterly contradict that. He finds a way for the two of them to be in his room alone. He invites her to sleep with him, and when she refuses, he overpowers and rapes her. Immediately afterwards he is filled with hatred for her, commanding an attendant to *Send this thing out of my presence*. Having had her, he is now repulsed by her. She has been fully objectified and now needs to be discarded.

The story began with Amnon declaring his love for Tamar. But had he genuinely loved her, this whole grotesque episode would never have happened. He had intense feelings for her, for sure. He was infatuated. But he was not being driven by love.

This is an extremely unpleasant example, but it makes a vital point. Our feelings can be a dreadful guide to what is loving behaviour. C.S. Lewis once wrote that "love begins to be a demon the moment he begins to be a god". He explains:

> *Every human love, at its height, has a tendency to claim for itself a divine authority. Its voice tends to sound as if it were the will of God Himself. It tells us not to count the cost, it demands of us a total commitment, it attempts to override all other claims and insinuates that any action which is done "for love's sake" is thereby lawful and even meritorious.*[39]

What Amnon interpreted as love would certainly have felt like a divine authority. It is why we need much more to go on than our feelings.

There are lots of times when the Bible says we shouldn't sleep with someone. Let's say it is two biological siblings, and they have started to recognise that they are romantically attracted to one another. The Bible is clear that this would not be an appropriate context for any kind of sexual or romantic relationship. But that is not the same as saying they can't love each other. It is simply saying that the way they are *wanting* to love each other is not actually how they have

---

39 C.S. Lewis, *The Four Loves* (HarperCollins, 2002), p 7-8.

been *designed* to love each other. If, in this instance, they are obedient to God, they will end up loving each other far better than if they gave full vent to their romantic desires.

This will always be the case with God. His restrictions on when it is appropriate to be sexually involved with someone will always be grounded in what is truly going to be best for those concerned. That means there will be times when, for the sake of loving someone better, we will have to say no to some of the ways we desire to express love for someone.

This is going to be the case for all of us at various points. Virtually all of us will find ourselves attracted to people whom God says we shouldn't sleep with. All of us have to say no to certain romantic and sexual desires. It's not because we're against love—it's because we're for it, in the right sense.

It is precisely at these times of tension that we tend to wonder if God really does know what he's talking about. The apostle John can help us once again. A few verses before writing about God being love, he wrote:

> *This is how we know what love is: Jesus Christ laid down his life for us.*   1 JOHN 3 v 16

You want proof that God really is love? Then look at the death of Jesus. Truly. When you understand that, you realise there never was and never will be an expression of love greater than that.

There's another way in which God helps us love one another.

On one occasion Jesus was asked which of the Old Testament commandments was the most important. Jews had calculated that there were over 600 individual commands in the Old Testament. So the question may be a way of asking which of these matters the most. What's the actual bottom line?

This is Jesus' answer:

> *"The most important one,"* answered Jesus, *"is this:*
> *'Hear, O Israel: The Lord our God, the Lord is one.*
> *Love the Lord your God with all your heart and with*
> *all your soul and with all your mind and with all*
> *your strength.' The second is this: 'Love your neigh-*
> *bour as yourself.' There is no commandment greater*
> *than these."* MARK 12 v 29-31

Both parts of Jesus' answer are quotations from the Old Testament. Jesus is not so much lifting these two commandments out as particular favourites as saying that they embody the whole law. God's commands are not just random-fire requirements that are unrelated to each other. They cohere and integrate into a particular shape. They are of a piece—they, like God, are "one". That shape Jesus sums up in the two commandments he cites.

Both are commandments to love: God, with all that we are and our neighbour, as we love ourselves. Again, God is all about love. This is what he wants from us. We are designed to live lives of love. Ultimate reality is not grounded in cold submission to an authoritarian deity but in heartfelt response to the God who wants his universe pulsating with love.

But that means seeing that these two dimensions of love go together. They reinforce and play off and depend on each other. They are not pulling us in two different directions. They go together.

This means we cannot consistently champion being loving towards others while being indifferent to God. Nor can we claim to be about loving God if we are careless in how we treat others. What we do with other human beings we are doing to the image of God himself. If we abuse someone, it is the likeness of God we are abusing. It is why all wrongdoing against other people is in fact wrongdoing against God.

But the reverse is also true, and no less challenging. Our attempts to love others will always be hindered if we have no relationship with the God who made them. We cannot succeed fully in love for our neighbour without love for God. The summary Jesus gives of the law is twofold because those two elements belong together. We can't truly have one without the other.

4. Love may need to wait

The Song of Songs in the Old Testament is a series of poetic exchanges between two young lovers. We see them meeting, getting to know each other, falling for each other, finally marrying and enjoying the thrill of their sexual consummation. It might surprise some people that such literature exists in the Bible. In fact it forms part of the Old Testament known as "wisdom" literature. It is designed to be instructive rather than titillating. We are meant to learn from it about the ways of love and desire.

One such lesson is found early on in the book. The book opens with the woman wanting to be kissed on the lips by this young man. His hand is under her head, and they are embracing (Song of Songs 2 v 6). Just as things are looking as if they are starting to heat up, they take (for us) an unexpected turn. The woman makes an oath before her friends and community:

> *Daughters of Jerusalem, I charge you*
> *by the gazelles and by the does of the field:*
> *Do not arouse or awaken love*
> *until it so desires.* SONG OF SONGS 2 v 7

We are given the image of a gazelle and a doe—two animals

known for both beauty and fertility, and therefore associated with lovemaking.[40] Though it's an apt picture for where
things seem to be heading with this couple, she has a warning for her friends. When it comes to love, there is an essential element of timing: we must not stir up or awaken love
"until it so desires".

Again, the imagery here is significant. Love is something
that can be aroused and awakened, and this needs to happen
at the right time—which means it is all too possible for it to
happen at the wrong time.

This sounds very alien to our typical way of thinking. By
and large, we tend to encourage sexual gratification in the
Western world. Everything is designed to arouse and stir up
romantic and sexual feelings as quickly as possible. We are
encouraged not to wait at all.

But the warning of this woman is vital. Romantic or sexual
love, by implication, can be difficult to restrain or control
once awakened. There is something about this desire which
we need to tread very carefully around. We tend to think it
can be switched on and off by our own control, but this ancient wisdom claims otherwise. Sexual feelings are meant to
produce something that is non-reversible. They are as powerful as they are for good reason: God has given them to us
to bind two people together at the very deepest level, in a
way that is not designed to be undone. We mustn't start the
process if it is not the right time.

WAKE UP AND SMELL THE (BURNT) COFFEE

For a number of years I worked in an old-fashioned family-
run coffee shop. One of my duties was to roast the coffee
beans in house. We stocked a couple of dozen varieties of

---

40 Philip Ryken, *Song of Songs* (Crossway, 2019), p 54.

coffee bean, many of which needed to be roasted quite differently. Most could be roasted without much attendance, but one particular variety—Robusta beans from Indonesia, if I recall—needed constant attention. There was a very precise moment at which they were done, and if they were left for just a moment or two longer, they would often catch fire, and the whole batch would go up in flames.

Timing matters. Roast Robusta coffee beans too long and you can ruin the whole thing. Awaken love too soon and it can have the same effect. What is meant to be deeply pleasurable becomes highly destructive, and we find ourselves in the midst of great pain and heartache. Sexual intimacy is precious. It needs to be shared with the right person at the right time. The wrong person at the wrong time, or even the right person at the wrong time, can be disastrous.

It is easy to dismiss the Christian view of sexuality by saying it is anti-love. But that is also a very shallow way to think. Love is too important to leave to simplistic soundbites. It matters, and so we need to understand it. People matter, and so we need to learn how to truly love one another. And the best way to do that is to follow the words of the God who is himself love.

God cares who we sleep with because he cares that we really do love each other well, and that might mean loving in a different way to how we feel. But there is another layer to this. God also cares that we know *his* love. Just as our love for one another is bound up with our love for him, so too human sexuality is designed to be bound up with God's love for us. In fact, it is meant to be a signpost to it.

Why does this really matter to God? The bigger story

I t's not often a world event happens only five miles from my front door. For people living in London or Washington, D.C., this might be a normal occurrence. But I live in a somewhat nondescript town. Some of the people who live here don't even seem to have heard of it. But the next-door town is much more famous—Windsor.

When Prince Harry married Meghan Markle in the grounds of Windsor Castle, needless to say, it was a bit of a big deal. I was in the States at the time, managing to miss all the action happening in my own neighbourhood, but coverage saturated the global media. People in the US were waking up early to have special royal-wedding viewing parties, complete with glasses of champagne at 6 o'clock in the morning.

A FAIRYTALE WEDDING

Everything about the day looked like a fairy tale: the sun shone brightly; Windsor Castle provided an iconic backdrop. Royalty was everywhere—and not just the British kind: the place was teeming with entertainment aristocracy as A-list Tinseltown VIPs and global rock stars arrived and took their places. The bride herself was a stunning Hollywood actress, and so this was celebrity-royalty and good old-fashioned blood royalty coming together as one. Hollywood was now officially part of the British monarchy.

Watching the coverage from just over four thousand miles away, it struck me that we Brits do this sort of thing really well. We no longer have an empire to boast about. When the Queen confers honours on her most worthy subjects, they are given titles like "Commander of the British Empire" and "Master of the British Empire"—which sounds grand until you remember that our empire is little more than some straggly sheep in the South Atlantic. We're not the global leader we once were.

But when it comes to pomp, we know what we're doing. Ceremony, processions, brassy fanfares, solemn vows, robed clerics, stunning gowns, chests puffed out to accommodate racks of medals, aircraft fly-bys—it all happens flawlessly and with precision timing. This is what we Brits *do*. It's not surprising that it makes for a global television event.

But what made this occasion so compelling was the heady combination of royalty *and romance*. A glamorous prince who seemed to have found the love of his life: someone who is his match and counterpart in all the ways that matter. Throw in some horse-drawn carriages, some crowns and George Clooney, and the whole planet turns up to watch. It seems to capture our imagination like nothing else.

WHAT TOOK YOU SO LONG?

Two people who seem made for each other finally getting together seems so right. People at weddings often tease the couple by saying, "What took you so long?!" There almost seems to be an urgency to it all. In the words of another Harry—the romantic lead from *When Harry Met Sally*— "When you realise you want to spend the rest of your life with somebody, you want the rest of your life to start as soon as possible".[41] There's something so elemental, so deeply and profoundly right about this that we daren't wait. A script somewhere deep within us is telling us that this is supremely significant. Romantic fulfilment is spoken of in quasi-apocalyptic language. In the language of *Jerry Maguire*, we're looking for the person who will complete us.

In classic romantic stories, the great happy ending is always the moment the couple get together. Harry realises he is truly in love with Sally and discovers she feels the same way. Or the will-they-won't-they couple definitively decide they *will*. Or the seemingly never-lucky-in-love guy or girl finally meets the person with whom they can succeed.

It's the sort of story we've seen, read and heard a thousand times. But behind all these stories is the assumption that the real story ends once the couple are at last together. That moment of mutual realisation, or when they have finally made it up the aisle together, is when the camera pans back and the story reaches its conclusion. That they have found each other is all we need to know. The journey is the fraught part; once they arrive at the destination, we can leave them, happy in our knowledge that they have made it there.

But the fact is, even the most dreamily romantic of us knows that it is not that simple. Once the couple get together, there is no automatic "happy ever after". The stories we've heard from the youngest of ages tells us there is, but life in the real world shows us otherwise. Even in the most

---

41 *When Harry Met Sally*, 1989.

successful romantic partnerships there is hard work. There are difficult times. There are stresses and strains. Hot tears are shed.

When I was a little boy, my great-grandparents' anniversary made it onto the local news. They'd been married for over 75 years. Such milestones are even rarer now. We just don't expect romance and marriage to last that long. We are surrounded by divorces and break-ups.

Yet something in us still thrills at the moment a couple get together. It seems to represent a promise that stirs something in all of us, married or not, happily or not. Despite all the realities of life we see around us, we find it hard to shake the notion that there is a love out there that can fix everything—fix even us. So even when it is someone else's marriage, this hope can still awaken within us. We know that real life doesn't work like this, but somewhere deep down we can't abandon the notion that it's somehow *meant* to.

A GALACTIC ROMANCE

The Christian faith has a very simple explanation for this. The story of the universe—of who God is and what he is doing in this world—is actually a romance.

Admittedly, that's not how it has often been presented. If you've encountered Christianity at all, it may have felt as if the message is that we all need to be more religious or ethical or spiritual, none of which sounds like the basis for a Nora Ephron or Nicholas Sparks movie.

But that's not what Christianity is about. It's the wrong framework, because when Jesus burst onto the first-century scene, one of the first ways he described himself was as something very surprising.

THE BRIDEGROOM

> *Now John's disciples and the Pharisees were fasting.*
> *Some people came and asked Jesus, "How is it that*
> *John's disciples and the disciples of the Pharisees are*
> *fasting, but yours are not?" Jesus answered, "How can*
> *the guests of the bridegroom fast while he is with them?*
> *They cannot, so long as they have him with them. But*
> *the time will come when the bridegroom will be taken*
> *from them, and on that day they will fast."*
>
> MARK 2 v 18-20

Jesus imagines two sorts of wedding scenes: one where the bridegroom is happily present and one where the bridegroom has been taken away by someone. In the first, the presence of the groom is the cause of celebration. When we are at a wedding reception, it is fitting not only to eat and drink but to enjoy doing so. It's where we let ourselves off the diet we've been on, and eat the sort and amount of food that wouldn't be typical for 4 p.m. on a Saturday afternoon. They're getting *married*. It is not the time for abstaining or being morose. That would actually be rude. Our hosts and the couple *want* us to celebrate.

The second kind of wedding scene that Jesus describes is one where the groom has been forcibly taken from the wedding party. It is hard for us to imagine this; it sounds more like a far-fetched movie than anything we can imagine really happening. But we can still picture the scene. Unknown assailants crash into the wedding and bundle the groom off at gunpoint, screeching away at high speed. The wedding feast is now over—the groom is gone. You're not going to pause for a moment and then go, "*Huh?* Anyway, back to the food everyone!" and carry on stuffing your face. Now is not the time.

To start gorging again would be wildly inappropriate. What was at the centre of all the celebrations has been taken away.

In the ancient world, fasting wasn't so much a medical activity as a spiritual one. Fasting was an expression of deep grief. When someone is deeply troubled, they lose their appetite. It is hard to eat when we are in despair and deep grief. And the same is true of spiritual grief. In the Old Testament, when someone was particularly aware of how they had turned away from the God who loves them, it was fitting to express remorse by fasting. By the time of Jesus, it had become a common spiritual discipline. There were regularly scheduled times in which you were supposed to reflect on your sin and grieve appropriately. Hence the surprise in this passage that Jesus' friends were not fasting like other people.

Jesus' point in response was to say that they were not fasting as normal because this particular moment of time was not normal. Jesus is saying, *You're in the middle of a wedding party. This is not the time for being gloomy. Glasses should be raised, and plates should be full.*

The implied reason for this is very clear. Jesus the Bridegroom is here. The violent removal of the groom will be the time to fast—a hint of what Jesus knew was going to happen to him in the near future. But now, while he is around, they should be rejoicing and celebrating.

That Jesus identified himself in this way was hugely significant. It was not random or arbitrary. Jesus was actually locating himself in a much bigger story—one that his contemporaries would have been familiar with. This idea of a spiritual groom coming to the people of God had a famous backstory, as we're about to see.

Why does this really matter to God? The better story

I grew up somewhat obsessed with the original *Star Wars* movies. It was a matter of pride for me and my friends that we knew virtually all the scripts off by heart. It was our shared vernacular. If a menacing teacher walked past us at school, one of us just needed to quietly make the sound of deep, metallic breathing and the rest of us would immediately get the reference—that the teacher was like a certain Sith Lord. If you weren't familiar with *Star Wars,* it wouldn't make sense. But for those of us that were, even half a second of that sound effect would be instantly understood as a reference to it.

Many of the contemporaries of Jesus knew the Jewish Scriptures in the way I know *Star Wars*. It was the script they'd grown up with and had learnt much of it by heart. It was their vernacular. So Jesus dropping references about himself being "the bridegroom" would have been very obviously loaded for his original listeners. Jesus was not saying, *I'm a bit like a bridegroom; people should celebrate while I'm around*; he was saying, *I am the bridegroom*, and everyone would have known what he meant.

Bridegroom—there's a story behind that word.

Actually, it is hinted at in the very first sentence of the Bible:

> *In the beginning God created the heavens and the*
> *earth.* GENESIS 1 v 1

There's lots packed into that short line: the universe is not an accident; there was a beginning, and before that beginning began, there was a God who willed us all into existence. But tucked away, very subtly, is a clue as to what this story is going to be about. Ancient Hebrew (in which the Old Testament was written) was like many other languages in that it gave nouns a gender. "Heaven" is masculine and "earth" is feminine.[42] The Bible opens with this "couple", and our expectation is that they're meant for each other. As the account of creation unfolds, we soon encounter another pairing: male and female (Genesis 1 v 27). They too belong together, and in the next chapter the first people we actually meet—Adam and Eve—*do* get together. And their getting together becomes a foretaste of the eventual and inevitable marriage of heaven and earth. This is what the whole Bible will be about.

As the Old Testament unfolds, we see that the relationship God intends to have with his people is a marriage. He presents himself not just as the superpower in the sky to whom all must submit, but as a groom who has come to win a people to himself. And his people are not just his fanbase or underlings; they are his *bride*—albeit a somewhat flaky and unfaithful one.

This is suggested throughout the Old Testament, but certain places make it explicit and linger over it.

---

42 Glen Scrivener, *Love Story: The Myth that Really Happened* (10 Publishing, 2017), p 10.

A DIVINE WEDDING

Psalm 45 is one example. It describes a glorious royal wedding—even better than Harry and Meghan's. We have the most glorious groom:

> *You are the most excellent of men*
> *and your lips have been anointed with grace,*
> *since God has blessed you forever.*
> *Gird your sword on your side, you mighty one;*
> *clothe yourself with splendour and majesty...*
> *You love righteousness and hate wickedness;*
> *therefore God, your God, has set you above your*
> *companions by anointing you with the oil of joy.*
>
> PSALM 45 v 2-3, 7

This groom is gracious and mighty, righteous and joyful. No wonder God has anointed and chosen him. The bride, too, is stunning:

> *Let the king be enthralled by your beauty ...*
> *People of wealth will seek your favour.*
> *All glorious is the princess within her chamber;*
> *her gown is interwoven with gold.*
> *In embroidered garments she is led to the king;*
> *her virgin companions follow her—*
> *those brought to be with her.*
> *Led in with joy and gladness,*
> *they enter the palace of the king.*   PSALM 45 v 11-15

This is the perfect couple, and it will be a sensational union. The psalm speaks of them having a family that will stretch out for generations and be celebrated across the world (v 17).

But there's a twist. And it's to do with the groom. There's more to him than we realise—not in a scandalous way but in a wonderful way. The writer of the psalm describes the ways in which God has lavished blessing on this man:

> *Your throne, O God, will last for ever and ever;*
> *a sceptre of justice will be the sceptre of your kingdom.*
> *You love righteousness and hate wickedness;*
> *therefore God, your God, has set you above your*
> *   companions*
> *by anointing you with the oil of joy.*
>
> PSALM 45 v 6-7

The character of this man is such that God has shown him great favour. He has proved his moral integrity, and God has blessed him. The groom seems amazing. Perhaps almost too amazing...

Because then the writer addresses the groom in an astonishing way:

> *Your throne, O God, will last for ever and ever.*
>
> PSALM 45 v 6

This royal groom is both (1) the one who God blesses, and (2) the eternal God himself. That he can be both identified with God and at the same time the recipient of blessing from God reflects what we saw earlier: that God is three Persons in loving relationship.

But the main point for us to see is that this groom is not only royal (as if that wasn't already enough to have going for him) but also divine. God is a bridegroom, and the bride of this psalm is actually a picture of his people.

Here are just a few similar examples:

> *Your Maker is your husband,*
> *The Lord Almighty is his name;*

And the Holy One of Israel is your redeemer,
he is called the God of all the earth.   ISAIAH 54 v 5

As a bridegroom rejoices over his bride,
so will your God rejoice over you.   ISAIAH 62 v 5

I will betroth you to me for ever;
*   I will betroth you in righteousness and justice,*
*   in love and compassion.*
I will betroth you in faithfulness,
*   and you will acknowledge the LORD.*
                                              HOSEA 2 v 19-20

I gave you my solemn oath and entered into a covenant
with you, declares the sovereign Lord, and you became
mine.   EZEKIEL 16 v 8

God is the groom; his people are the bride. One of the great refrains all through the Bible is, "You shall be my people, and I will be your God." This is the language of mutual belonging, of covenant love.

Against this backdrop, it becomes clear what Jesus means by referring to himself as "the bridegroom". He is not claiming to be *like* a groom in some way, but to be the *ultimate* groom. He is claiming to be the covenant-making God, who has promised to make a people for himself and to give himself to them as a husband gives himself to his bride.

This trajectory continues forward into the New Testament as well. The letters that form the bulk of it keep drawing their readers to the way in which Jesus is the groom to his people. The apostle Paul, for example, can say:

> *For it is said, "The two will become one flesh." But*
> *whoever is united with the Lord is one with him in*
> *spirit.*   1 CORINTHIANS 6 v 16-17

We've seen "the two will become one flesh" from Genesis 2 already. Paul is saying that just as the husband and wife become one flesh, so Jesus and those who believe in him are one spirit.

Paul makes this most explicit in a passage addressed to husbands and wives:

> *"For this reason a man will leave his father and*
> *mother and be united to his wife, and the two will*
> *become one flesh." This is a profound mystery – but I*
> *am talking about Christ and the church.*
>   EPHESIANS 5 v 31-32

MARKING THE ROUTE

Last week I had the chance to hike on one of my favourite English mountains with a couple of American friends. Every now and then we came across a prominent stack of stones by the path, so I explained that these are cairns—waypoints designed to mark the route when there is low visibility or when snow is covering the path.

This is what passages like this are for us—markers reminding us of what reality is ultimately about, and of where all history is finally heading.

The very ending of the Bible also speaks in this way. Speaking in very figurative language, the book of Revelation describes the final wedding feast of God and his people, the Lamb (Jesus) and his Bride:

Let us rejoice and be glad
 and give him glory!
For the wedding of the Lamb has come,
 and his bride has made herself ready.
Fine linen, bright and clean,
 was given her to wear.   REVELATION 19 v 7-8

Believe it or not, this is how the Bible describes the end of the world: the long-anticipated wedding of God and his bride. The whole Bible is a romance.

MARRIAGE SIGNS

This has actually had a deep impact on the way we typically do weddings in the West. Many of the things we associate with a traditional wedding ceremony were developed to ensure our earthly weddings reflected the heavenly one described in the Bible. Here are some examples:[43]

- *The groom arrives first and waits for his bride to come.* He has already won her and now he has everything ready in advance so that all she needs to do is arrive.
- *Her arrival is a big deal—intentionally so.* Everyone makes sure they're already there and ready so that they don't miss this. When she walks in everyone looks. Nobody's eyes are on the groom. The bride is radiant. Her dress is white and spotless. She looks amazing.
- *She is presented to him as his bride.* They make lifelong, exclusive, covenant promises to one another. They exchange rings as a sign of those promises, and a legal declaration is made that they are now married.

---

43   For an excellent and short video on this, see vimeo.com/213704872 (Accessed 1st October 2019).

- *What is hers becomes his, and what is his becomes hers.* All that they have belongs to each other. In many cases she takes on his name.
- *Later on they physically consummate their marriage.*

This choreography is deliberate. At each point it echoes something about the relationship Jesus has with his people.

- Jesus is the one who has gone ahead and prepared everything in heaven and made it ready for us.
- His death and resurrection for us wipe away all our sin so that we can be presented as beautiful and spotless.
- We are given to him, and enter an eternal, exclusive, covenant relationship with him. He is pledged to us, and we to him, forsaking all others.
- Our union is legal. What belongs to him is now ours. We receive his perfect righteousness. What is ours belongs to him. He takes on our imperfection and sin.
- We now take on his name. We're identified as followers of Christ. That is our new identity.

So for Christians, marriage has a purpose for and benefit to the husband and wife, but it also has the wider purpose and public benefit of being a shadow and foretaste of what God is offering to all people in Jesus.

God has given us this whole dimension in life—making us sexual beings and giving us this instinct towards lifelong partnership—precisely to point us to the deeper and greater reality of his covenant love for us in Christ. This dimension to life, like all others, is distorted and diminished by our having turned from God. Our sexual feelings are disordered and often inappropriate; we don't keep our promises; we make sex about fulfilling our own appetites. But the basic shape remains. Our sexuality is meant to point us to the deeper yearning, the fuller satisfaction, and the greater consummation that comes from knowing Jesus.

This being so, it is easy to see how we can mistake marriage and romantic fulfillment for the reality it is designed to point us to. We sense there is something profound and meaningful that is meant to be discovered there. But rather than seeing it as a sign of something greater, we mistake it for the reality itself.

MISTAKEN IDENTITY

There's a scene in the movie *Amadeus* where the young Mozart meets Emperor Joseph II for the first time. As he is led in, he is presented before a man who is dressed grandly and looks to be highly important, so Mozart instinctively bows low, thinking him to be the emperor. The man looks horrified and discreetly points towards the side of the room where the *actual* emperor is sitting at a piano. It is an awkward moment as Mozart realises what he has done, and he quickly goes on to acknowledge the real emperor appropriately.

Many of us need to go through a similar process when it comes to marriage and romance. When we first encounter it, it can seem so glorious and resplendent with significance that we easily think it must be ultimate. How else do we account for how it can make us feel? But the fact remains that it is the purpose of such things to point us to where fulfilment is really meant to be found.

One of the ways that happens is when we realise that our relationships cannot deliver all that we expect from them. If we look to them to provide ultimate satisfaction, we will only be disappointed. Once again, C.S. Lewis puts it so vividly:

> *We are half-hearted creatures, fooling about with drink and sex and ambition when infinite joy is offered us,*

> *like an ignorant child who wants to go on making*
> *mud pies in a slum because he cannot imagine what*
> *is meant by the offer of a holiday at the sea. We are far*
> *too easily pleased.*[44]

To make sexual freedom our ultimate good is to think that sex and romance is simply an end in itself.

But if we realise that our fascination with romance is actually a memory-trace of a deeper story—an echo of a greater tune, a signpost to the ultimate destination—then we will find the reality that can transcend even the most intimate of relationships we can experience.

WHY DOES GOD CARE WHO I SLEEP WITH?

This is what God invites us to do. It's why he cares who we sleep with. It's why *we* care who we sleep with. Our sexuality is meant to tell a story: the greatest story because it's all about the greatest love—the love God has shown us in Jesus Christ.

A Christian friend of mine who experiences same-sex attraction has written about how the sexual ethic of the Bible is, in some respects, "an inconvenient truth". And yet she can write that she believes in "a greater truth than my small mind can fathom, a deeper desire than my weak heart can muster, and a closer relationship than the best human marriage can attain".[45]

Each of us has our own story to tell when it comes to this issue, with our own unique ups and downs. I mentioned in the introduction that I'm single and therefore (as a Christian) sexually abstinent. What I didn't mention is that the

---

44 C. S. Lewis, "The Weight of Glory" in *The Weight of Glory and Other Addresses* (HarperCollins, 2001), p 26.

45 Rebecca McLaughlin, *Confronting Christianity: 12 Hard Questions for the World's Largest Religion* (Crossway, 2019), p 155.

only romantic and sexual attractions I've ever had have been towards other men. Many would assume that the Christian sexual ethic couldn't possibly work for someone in my situation, having to say no to these desires and being single long-term. And yet so many of us, like and unlike me, have found the teaching of Jesus to be a better story to live by.

The fact that the question at the heart of this book is asked at all, let alone so urgently—reflects that we're thinking of sex both *too much* and *too little*.

Too much because we're tempted to find our deepest fulfilment in sexual intimacy.

Too little because we are missing what our deepest sexual and romantic yearnings are meant to be pointing us to.

We care about who we sleep with because we sense something significant hinges on this. It does. But it tends not to be the something we were expecting. Our sexuality as human beings is meant to speak to us of the "greater truth", "deeper desire" and "closer relationship" that my friend writes about above. *God* cares who we sleep with because he cares who we spend eternity with, and he wants us to know him and experience his ultimate love for ever.

It is why the Christian understanding of sex is actually good news—for those (like me) for whom it means remaining celibate for as long as I am unmarried; for those who are married for whom it means being faithful and servant-hearted in sexual conduct; for all of us for whom this message can land with an uncomfortable challenge.

For all of us it is a message not primarily concerned with what we do and don't do with our genitals (though it has significant things to say about this), but with who we will ultimately give our hearts to, and where we will look for our deepest experience of love.

Acknowledgements

It has been a privilege to be invited to write this book and contribute to this particular series.

The Good Book Company has been a great pleasure to work with once again. Tim Thornborough has been incredibly patient, bearing with me as I missed deadline after deadline. Thank you, Tim, for all your support and good grace. The book would be much poorer without his suggestions and feedback. Austin Wilson continues to be indispensable in all sorts of ways. I should also thank Andrew Wilson, from whom I stole the title.

A number of people were an invaluable help in reading various parts of the manuscript or giving advice at various stages: Rebecca McLaughlin and Glen Scrivener both fed in great ideas at key moments. But special thanks must go to my RZIM colleague Lou Philips, who not only read the entire manuscript but was a consistent encouragement over many months, especially when morale was low.

The wonderful home of the Roe family in Shincliffe, County Durham, was, as always, a great place to do the bulk of the writing. I am deeply thankful for their hospitality.

This book is one of a series published under the auspices of the Zacharias Institute in Atlanta, Georgia, and the Oxford Centre for Christian Apologetics in the UK. It is a huge pleasure and privilege to be associated with these bodies, and to be part of the wonderful team at Ravi Zacharias International Ministries.

Can science explain everything? Many people think so. Science, and the technologies it has spawned, has delivered so much to the world: clean water; more food; better healthcare; longer life. And we live in a time of rapid scientific progress that holds enormous promise for many of the problems we face as humankind. So much so, in fact, that many see no need or use for religion and belief systems that offer us answers to the mysteries of our universe. Science has explained it, they assume. Religion is redundant.

Oxford Maths Professor and Christian believer John Lennox offers a fresh way of thinking about science and Christianity that dispels the common misconceptions about both. He reveals that not only are they *not* opposed, but they can and must work together to give us a fuller understanding of the universe and the meaning of our existence.

"This book is a remarkable achievement: engaging with all the big issues in just a few pages, while remaining profound, accessible, engaging and, to my mind, completely compelling."

Vaughan Roberts
Author, speaker and pastor

thegoodbook.co.uk | thegoodbook.com
thegoodbook.com.au | thegoodbook.co.nz | thegoodbook.co.in

Is Jesus
History?

JOHN DICKSON

What can we really know for sure about the past? Can anything from ancient history be regarded as fact? In particular, how seriously can we take the historical sources for the life, death and resurrection of Jesus of Nazareth? Did he really even live in first-century Galilee and Judaea, or is he a figure of legend?

In this timely book, historian Dr John Dickson unpacks how the field of history works, giving readers the tools to evaluate for themselves what we can confidently say about figures like the Emperor Tiberius, Alexander the Great, Pontius Pilate and, of course, Jesus of Nazareth. He presents the conclusions of mainstream scholars—both Christian and not—and asks some pertinent contemporary questions, without offering any pushy answers. If Jesus really did exist, what are we to make of his own claims and those of his followers, and what would any of it mean for us today?

> *"An eminently readable and relevant introduction that debunks many misconceptions about the gospel accounts of Jesus."*

Dr David Wenham
Historian, author; Tutor, Wycliffe Hall, Oxford.

thegoodbook.co.uk | thegoodbook.com
thegoodbook.com.au | thegoodbook.co.nz | thegoodbook.co.in

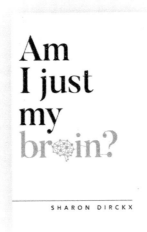

Am
I just
my
br in?

SHARON DIRCKX

Modern research is uncovering more and more detail of what our brain is and how it works. We are living, thinking creatures who carry around with us an amazing organic supercomputer in our heads. But what is the relationship between our brains and our minds—and ultimately our sense of identity as a person? Are we more than machines? Is free-will an illusion? Do we have a soul?

Brain-imaging scientist Dr Sharon Dirckx lays out the current understanding of who we are from biologists, philosophers, theologians and psychologists, and points towards a bigger picture that suggests answers to the fundamental questions of our existence. Not just "What am I?" but "Who am I?"—and "Why am I?"

"Fresh, clear and helpful, Dirckx opens up a key part of what has been called the most important conversation of our time. Is freedom only a fiction? Is human dignity merely a form of 'speciesism'? Are we no more than our brains? The answers to such questions affect us all, and it is vital that we all explore them."

Os Guinness
Author and speaker

thegoodbook
COMPANY

thegoodbook.co.uk | thegoodbook.com
thegoodbook.com.au | thegoodbook.co.nz | thegoodbook.co.in

Thanks for reading this book. We hope you enjoyed it, and found it helpful.

Most people want to find answers to the big questions of life: Who are we? Why are we here? How should we live? But for many valid reasons we are often unable to find the time or the right space to think positively and carefully about them.

Perhaps you have questions that you need an answer for. Perhaps you have met Christians who have seemed unsympathetic or incomprehensible. Or maybe you are someone who has grown up believing, but need help to make things a little clearer.

At The Good Book Company, we're passionate about producing materials that help people of all ages and stages understand the heart of the Christian message, which is found in the pages of the Bible.

Whoever you are, and wherever you are at when it comes to these big questions, we hope we can help. As a publisher we want to help you look at the good book that is the Bible because we're convinced that as we meet the person who stands at its centre—Jesus Christ—we find the clearest answers to our biggest questions.

Visit our website to discover the range of books, videos and other resources we produce, or visit our partner site www.christianityexplored.org for a clear explanation of who Jesus is and why he came.

Thanks again for reading,

Your friends at The Good Book Company

thegoodbook.com | thegoodbook.co.uk
thegoodbook.com.au | thegoodbook.co.nz
thegoodbook.co.in

WWW.CHRISTIANITYEXPLORED.ORG

Our partner site is a great place to explore the Christian faith, with powerful testimonies and answers to difficult questions.